21

BLOOD PAPA

BLOOD PAPA

RWANDA'S NEW GENERATION

JEAN HATZFELD

TRANSLATED FROM THE FRENCH BY JOSHUA DAVID JORDAN

FARRAR, STRAUS AND GIROUX | NEW YORK

Farrar, Straus and Giroux
175 Varick Street, New York 10014

Printed in the United States of America
Originally published in French in 2015 by Éditions Gallimard, Paris,
    as *Un papa de sang*
English translation published in the United States by Farrar,
    Straus and Giroux
First American edition, 2018

Library of Congress Cataloging-in-Publication Data
Names: Hatzfeld, Jean, author. | Jordan, Joshua David, translator.
Title: Blood Papa : Rwanda's new generation / Jean Hatzfeld ; translated
    from the French by Joshua David Jordan.
Other titles: Papa de sang. English
Description: First American edition. | New York : Farrar, Straus and
    Giroux, 2018. | "Originally published in French in 2015 by Éditions
    Gallimard, Paris, as Un papa de sang."
Identifiers: LCCN 2018007632 | ISBN 9780374279783 (hardcover)
Subjects: LCSH: Genocide—Rwanda—History—20th century. |
    Tutsi (African people)—Crimes against—Rwanda—History—20th
    century. | Rwanda—History—Civil War, 1994—Personal narratives.
Classification: LCC DT450.435 .H38513 2018 | DDC 967.5710431—dc23
LC record available at https://lccn.loc.gov/2018007632

Designed by Richard Oriolo

www.fsgbooks.com
www.twitter.com/fsgbooks • www.facebook.com/fsgbooks

10   9   8   7   6   5   4   3   2   1

CONTENTS

MEMORY

THE PARENTS

THE FUTURE

MEMORY

THE MARSHES

ONCE THE BUSHES AND BRANCHES RISE HIGH enough to scrape the vehicle's top, we are driving in a green penumbra, stealing through what resembles a lush underground passage. But this is no adventure. We have already been down the now-overgrown road leading to Nganwa. At its end, on the hillside, lived Ignace Rukiramacumu. And there he is, right in front of us—Ignace, the man clad in peculiar calf-length pants. He scurries barefoot behind a young woman striding ahead, her hair covered in a very lovely yellow turban. He seems to be yelling at her. It is a surprise to find him here, since he should be breaking stones at a work camp some fifty kilometers away. He carries a bundle on his head and turns around at the sound of our car and laughs. His dry, time-creased face hasn't changed a bit since our last visit. More startling still is discovering the old trickster's wily gaze intact and the same sardonic look.

He tells us that he returned that very day from three years of work reeducation, fulfilling his *travaux d'intérêt général*, during which he cleared roadsides, crushed loose rock, and ate tins of sauceless beans. He was sixty-two years old at the time of the killings in 1994. His peers exempted him from the expeditions into the swamps, thinking the work too strenuous for his scrawny legs. This did nothing, however, to prevent him from poaching Tutsis. In the evenings, when the madness of the killings seemed finally to subside, he could be seen descending into the papyrus armed with the same bow he had once used to hunt waterfowl.

Upon his return from exile in Congo, he was imprisoned at the penitentiary in Rilima with the Kibungo gang, among whom he was the first to be released, thanks to a presidential pardon of older inmates. He came home scot-free. But ten years later his extravagant display of bad faith during the *gaçaça* trials earned him a sentence to the work camp.* Now, at eighty-one years old, he has served his time in prison, driven on, one gathers, by rank resentment.

The young woman with whom he is quarreling as we exchange news is not his daughter but his wife, Jeanne. On his way home today, he had gone to fetch her from the nearby *mudugudu* to which she had run away for a second time.† He had brought her home with him, we learn, because of all the gossip circulating about her in the work camp. Their argument resumes with full-throated yelling punctuated by mutual threats to wring the other's neck. There seems to be no stopping them. Finally, Ignace asks me to act as mediator. Jeanne scrupulously sizes me up, then accepts. The bottles of Primus in the trunk couldn't have come at a better time.‡

Gaçaça means "soft grass," the name for the people's courts held in the open air under the trees. Inspired by ancestral traditions, they were established to relieve a judicial system so weakened by the genocide that it was unable to handle the massive number of criminals standing trial.

†A *mudugudu* is a development of homes built as a collective. They emerged in the aftermath of the genocide as part of a government project designed to address the destruction of housing and to ensure greater security by bringing together communities otherwise isolated on the hills.

‡Primus is Rwanda's most popular beer. A Belgian brand brewed in Gisenyi, a town in the western part of the country, the inexpensive and slightly bitter beer is drunk unchilled (*ishyushye*) or, more rarely, cold (*ikonge*) straight from its 25-ounce bottles. It has increasingly been supplanted in Rwandan cities by other brands, such as Mützig or Amstel, which are more to contemporary tastes.

Ignace's house, a vast structure covered with beige tiles, preserves the memory of a former opulence despite the cracks in the walls and other stigmata of his incarcerations. He was a tireless farmer—his back bent over the earth on which his first wife exhausted herself—and an impressive innovator who owed his success to coffee crops.

We carry benches outside into the shade of the long, flowery branches of an *umunzenze* tree. The issue turns out to be simple. Ignace's captivity forced him to sell his best land to his daughters from a previous marriage. Jeanne received nothing from the sale save for the gibes and threats of the daughters, who lived next door, their eyes greedily fixed on the house. Jeanne, a woman who trudged across the country with her two children, seduced by the stout heart of a thriving widower and the promise of an immense plot of land, suddenly found herself alone. She feared losing all she had. So she took refuge in the *mudugudu*, settling in with a male friend, from whom she enjoyed more than basic hospitality. The power of love courses through her veins. She didn't know, she pleads, how long they were going to keep her husband in the camp. Ignace grumbles and jeers. He is surly, demanding unconditional surrender; she is stubborn, stipulating future guarantees on the land. The haggling promises to be long.

In the distance, one hears an animal's nagging yelps, which are too guttural for the dog or the serval one sometimes comes across. It has been droning its single note since we arrived, as if the beast has always been there. Its barks rise from the bottom of the valley. An injured animal stuck in the mud, perhaps, or haunting the depths of the marshes.

In a previous book I wrote about Ignace's house: "Built on a hill ridge in Nganwa, the house overlooks the Akanyaru River, rising above his land from a steep slope that affords one of the most magnificent panoramas in the region." Nothing has changed since then. Nowhere else can one take in such a sweeping view of the marshes—not from the hilly edge of Englebert's land, nor from the summit of the Cyugaro Forest, nor from the ridge path near Pancrace's place. Nowhere else do the marshes arouse such wonder.

At the field's end, thickets studded with yellow flowers cover winding red-earth gullies. Farther down, the bright green of banana groves and the celadon of palm trees are outlined by peat fires. The vastness of the marshes extends beyond, blanketing the Akanyaru River, whose almost motionless course one senses more than sees. A sea of foliage stretches to the first mountain foothills, which dissolve mistily at the horizon. The rolling bottle-green of the papyrus predominates, flecked with brightly colored reeds and silvery flashes from the ponds in which the morning sun reflects its dazzling rays. Right now, the sun blinds with a stifling light, but later, as it tips behind the skyline, it will gild the horizon with first an orangey yellow then an eerie pink glow.

Before I discovered the marshes, it was impossible for me to imagine the scenes of the manhunts that Jeannette Ayinkamiye and Francine Niyitegeka had described and, in particular, to understand how the two of them had lasted for so many weeks. Once I saw the marshes, it was hard to pull myself away; I returned to them constantly, staring mesmerized through moments of doubt and disgust.

It was Ignace who said to me one day, as we were discussing the marshes: "The corpses were rotting so quickly that we no longer recognized those we had struck. We came across death with nearly every step and yet we never imagined our own or that of our families. Death became at once routine and unreal. I mean, it left us untouched. The truth of the genocide is in the mouths of the killers, who manipulate and conceal it, and in the mouths of the dead, who have taken it away with them."

From where we sit, we hear, besides the yelps rising from the marshes, a background sound of herons' raspy barks, the shriller squawks of white vultures gliding overhead, ibises' bursts of laughter, and a concert of less distinct songs, perhaps parrots or tiny talapoin monkeys, which, they say, live here in throngs. As one approaches the muddy water, the cries are lost in the din of screeching frogs and egrets, of grunts and whirs. With a bit of luck, one spots a herd of warthogs wading at the edge of a pond and, more rarely, the raised head of a sitatunga antelope swimming in the brackish water. White waterlilies are lulled by the current. Pink orchids fringe islets of reeds. There, in the sludge, lie the families of Berthe and Claudine, Francine's baby, Innocent's parents and sister, Jeannette's mother, Angélique's parents, Jean-Baptiste's wife and son, and Edith's parents and parents-in-law. Thousands of bodies have sunk into the Akanyaru and Akagera marshes, which are haunted now by a crowd of ghosts who climb the hills to torment the living.

IT HAS BEEN nineteen years since the killings: the age of an adolescent. I know many young people who have grown up in the company of these revenants. Each has had to sort out the history for themselves, a history that is now a part of them. I met several to write this book—children of the survivors and of the killers who spoke in my previous books. They all know the marshes, which come into view as one crosses the long bridge at the entrance to the district of Nyamata. They all know the marshes' evil secrets.

Only one of them has ventured out alone to the brownish water's edge to see the swamps up close and to give form to what he has heard described since childhood. His name is Jean-Pierre

Habimana, one of Alphonse Hitiyaremye's sons. His father is Ignace's friend and a killer from the gang in *Machete Season*. A nice boy, Jean-Pierre lives in Nyamabuye, on a hillside along the Akagera River. He is finishing his tailor's apprenticeship in a workshop near the Kabukuba market. Here, in a few words, is how he describes his "awkward childhood."

JEAN-PIERRE HABIMANA

NINETEEN YEARS OLD

Son of Alphonse Hitiyaremye, former Hutu prisoner

MY SEVEN-YEAR-OLD LEGS CARRIED ME DOWN THE path to school. It was risky. I had to run nonstop because the other boys would single me out. Sometimes I would hear someone shout, "That one there's a killer's son. Everyone saw his father, how he swung the machete until his arms almost broke. Killing runs in his blood." But I couldn't turn back to look. Other times, I crossed paths with shorter kids who would spit at me, and I had to hide in the brush. Many adults pushed their children to harass and taunt us. I was afraid, which is understandable. In the school-yard, when we were playing ball, I might be attacked on all sides by survivors' kids. Because of my father, of course. They all knew he lived in prison. I kept my mouth shut—I knew that it would be better to wait for Papa's return before speaking up. Grumbling words rumbled from Tutsi lips. I was hit with stones. That lasted for two or three years, then peace suddenly smiled on me. The authorities lectured them to wait for the *gaçaças*, to stop plotting punishments for us. In class, the torments were over; the teachers meant business.

It was a childhood rife with worry. I would listen to the neighbors describe the war and their escape to Congo. I would also hear the noisy squabbles at the cabaret. For people around here, drinking pours out all the trouble of past ordeals. When drinkers get drunk, if they feel stung by the nasty things the other ethnicity has said or done, they go hard in their talk and quarrels come quick. The children huddle out of sight, and although they catch every word, nothing makes any sense.

Myself, I got up the courage to ask my brother a few careful questions. It was safer than being snubbed by the adults. He said he didn't know. I asked my mama why my papa had to stay in prison instead of taking his place in the family, like so many other papas had in theirs. She dodged the questions. She weaved her way through explanations. I think she feared that we'd overreact. It's risky raising children without a papa's strength.

On the hill, my friends didn't know any more than I did, and what they said didn't sound anything like the truth. It was mostly at school that I grasped the story of the killings. The teachers explained the genocide to us. They followed a history program developed by the authorities and gave straightforward answers to our questions. They spoke patiently. They said that Hutus had decimated Tutsis because of a harmful government. But they didn't give excuses the way the parents did.

Of course, no student even hinted at his own family's situation. It was forbidden to talk about one's papa or a schoolmate's. I visited the memorials with my class. I went back several times. I heard about the hunts under the papyrus in the marshes, and I wanted to go down to see where the Tutsis had actually hid for so long. I trailed behind the groups on pilgrimage to the swamps. I stayed silent to hear their memories. It was a big thing to behold the marshes, to listen to how it all took place: the hunting-party songs, the machetes' bloody blows, the muddy holes under the papyrus where people hid.

Our neighbors were something else. I didn't doubt that they

knew all about the killers' wicked deeds. How couldn't they know? But if I asked them, they'd sidestep anything exact. Except Mama. As I said, at first she seemed annoyed; she insisted on the government's misguided policies and repeated that the killers had had no choice. Then, one day, she tried her hand at the truth. I was twelve. She told me very plainly how my papa and his colleagues had killed Tutsis from the hills. She held nothing back about the blood on the blades. She explained that before the killings Papa hadn't looked anything like a killer: he was cheerful, he acted kindly in dealings with Tutsis, he was always among the first to lend others a hand in the fields. She described how well-off they were; how comfortably they lived, with no worries from the neighbors; and why, on the very first day of the killings, he left at the front of the group.

What did I learn? Basically, that my papa farmed a prosperous plot of land and did well in the drink business, too. His wealth earned him influence. Plus, people knew he was the adoptive son of the sector's warrant officer, which was very important in the neighbors' eyes. The two men strode proudly down the streets of Nyamabuye. By the time the killings came, he and the official had put all the preparations in place. It would have been unthinkable for the officer to lead the men into the marshes without his adoptive son by his side. The richest farmers had to set the example. To make a long story short, my papa's success prevented him from slipping to the back of the expeditions.

As she told me, Mama got angry at Papa no shortage of times. She somewhat accused him of being the cause of their hardships—even if she played with the words. She repeated that the militia turned up each morning at everyone's doors to make sure that everyone participated properly in the expeditions. It was only when the trials were supposed to start that she avoided blaming him too harshly. Which is understandable. As for me, I went to see my papa at the prison in Rilima every month. It was a five-hour bicycle ride; our conversations were kept to five minutes because of the jostling of the crowd. We exchanged timid words and bits of news. The prisoners' pink uniforms upset me. Among us children, we said our papas were being kept in Rilima out of revenge. We grumbled; we complained that their imprisonment was unfair. So, although we were young, Mama decided to set us straight. She told us that the high walls of Papa's prison were no injustice; he had gotten his hands dirty. She even told us how she had stepped in to keep him from joining the expeditions, how she had failed because he was very determined and worked up by the others.

MY NAME IS Jean-Pierre Habimana. Age: nineteen years old. My papa's name is Alphonse. He farms two plots of land in Nya-mabuye. My mama's name is Consolée. She also works as a farmer and supports her husband unfailingly. There are three of us brothers and one sister. My name means "offering to God." I'm a very devout Catholic. I love God. I served at mass wearing my altar boy robe, and I still do my best to assist the priests. Deep down, I think God somewhat forgot about Rwanda. Otherwise, how do you explain that He would allow the genocide to happen? Yet it is through God's grace that the killings didn't reach absolute zero. It's thanks to Him that some Tutsis still made it through the hell of the marshes and that some Hutus were pardoned and pushed to return humbly to their plots to pick up the hoe again. I believe that God saved these people so that His children could bear witness to His power to save. That strengthens my faith in Him.

WHAT DO I remember from the year of the genocide? Nothing. I was too little. We fled to Congo. I have heard many people speak badly about that time; I have negative impressions. In Congo, I think we lived in fear of war. We stayed in tents surrounded by the volcano's black rocks. People lived on top of one another in the camp. They squeezed into line to wait for sacks of grain. They sang. Would you like a specific memory? People sang without ever running out of breath. With no land to work, they formed choirs. I remember crystal-clear the return to the Bugesera on trucks so long we would never have known they existed. This was in '97. I had never ridden in a motor vehicle and not even on a bicycle. We stopped on a road, and someone told me that that was our hill.

I grew up in Nyamabuye. As I said, I ran all the way to school to avoid being picked on. In class, I regained my calm. The teachers fussed over me because I was very clever at math. I darted through problems, and everyone knew it. It was a breeze, to be honest; school opened its arms to me. For sports, I picked basketball because of all the kids trying out for soccer. I played it effortlessly, despite my modest height. People said I was a fearless dribbler.

Papa's imprisonment thwarted my education. Poverty drove me from school three times. I was expelled in my first year of secondary school. In my fifth, I had to quit while waiting for the *minerval* to be paid—in vain.* In my sixth year, I had to stop again, that time to learn carpentry at a technical school. I went for construction work over agriculture because the country's development offers more attractive prospects. I did an apprenticeship, I finished my internship, then I gave it up. I chose tailoring, like my sister, the one who makes suits in the yellow boutique on Nyamata's main

---

*A term deriving from Minerva, the goddess of wisdom, intelligence, and industry, *minerval* refers to the tuition for high schools and universities in Belgium, the Democratic Republic of the Congo, Rwanda, and Burundi. In Rwanda in the 1990s, tuition was very expensive for the children of farmers, who often had to interrupt their schooling because of poor harvests. Tuition has now decreased considerably or been eliminated in primary and secondary schools.

street. A tailor named Alexis took me on as his apprentice. He says he is pleased with my work. Refining my skills will take another year. I work in the Kabukuba market not far from Nyamata. I enjoy cutting fabric; this new line of work is less exhausting than construction. I need to find a humanitarian organization to sponsor the purchase of my sewing machine. The machine is special in that it lets you sew flowers and decorations on women's dresses. It's a rare thing in the Bugesera, a costly investment.

In my workshop, there are nine of us young tailors who work as a cooperative: five survivor children and four Hutus. We get along well. We lend each other a hand on the sewing machines; we share the chores in the living quarters. Everyone pitches in for food and takes turns preparing the meals. We watch movies on tape. Whoever is the most expert with internet introduces it to the others, if we have the time, and the ones who know the ins and outs of computers teach the group. We never speak of the genocide. Sometimes a dissatisfied customer blows his top: he hurls hateful words and brings up the genocide in a threatening tone of voice. We don't respond.

Anyway, I never mention the killings with coworkers from the other ethnicity. We don't talk about our parents. Sitting down with a survivor's son to talk to him about the dark times or ask him about his problems—that, I still haven't done. As for us, we were brought low by poverty and mistreated with nasty words. And yet our parents always watched over us. The humiliation will slip away in time; we won't be so old before we seem just like normal people. The survivors, though, have no family to stand by them as they grow up. They have no guidance to protect them. As children, they struggle to make their way through adult dangers. They suffer from abandonment as well as trauma. It really is a big thing.

· · ·

I **FEEL HUTU.** In Kabukuba, where I'm something like a foreigner, I can't always tell the difference between Hutu and Tutsi
faces. I would be happy to marry a Tutsi, even though I don't know
if there is one in the dry Bugesera who will have me. I know Tutsi
girls who are very fancy but no less cheerful. They aren't proud
like the ones from times past. I don't worry about ethnicity. In
many countries in Africa, ethnicity doesn't concern anyone; people
don't have any hang-up living with the ethnicity they were given at
birth. In Rwanda, it attracts misfortune and hinders understanding. People steer clear of it now. But can you feel ashamed of
being Hutu if that is your fate? Many people claim that ethnicity
has no place in Rwanda anymore, that in the future it will simply
disappear. I think that if we ignore such a natural truth, we distill
venom that is bound to poison children from a very young age. If
we bury ethnicity, confusion constantly inflames the frustration
of victims. I understand them. It's important for the ones who suffered to be clear about who suffered and who committed crimes.

No, I'm not tired of it all—I don't want to sweep it all away.
Because I pray. Being a Christian gives me the strength to accept
the disappointments I encounter in life. If, in that fateful month
of April, neighbors had sincerely believed that man was made in
God's image, they wouldn't have raised their machetes. Today we
aren't looking to forget, but I don't know what we are looking for.
The influence of the past isn't going to fade. Cutting down neighbors like animals is a big thing. People are going to keep talking
about and examining the genocide for generations to come, because
it is an unnatural history.

AT THE MARKET

WHAT LOVELIER ADVERTISEMENT FOR FABRICS than a beautiful woman dozing atop piles of multicolored cut cloth, dressed head to toe in matching hues. In the suffocating heat of the Nyamata market, Angélique slumbers in her boutique at the entry to the fabric aisle. She awakes, makes a contrite wave of the hand, then smiles. The smile is a pleasure to behold because the last time I saw her she was wandering the street, her face slightly swollen, her mood dark, and her head aching with nasty migraines.

Angélique Mukamanzi, still just a teenager at the time, told me shortly after the killings: "In Ntarama, survivors turn bad or desperate . . . There are plenty of men and women who no longer bother. As soon as they scrape together a little money, they drink Primus and let everything drop. They get drunk on alcohol and bad memories. There are some who get a kick out of retelling the same fateful moments . . . Nowadays, I see this wretched time that stretches out before me as an enemy. I suffer from being bound to the past and from a life that wasn't meant for me." She gazed bitterly at her palms hardened by the hoe.

In this new covered market, one is plunged into a crowd more hurried now than in the past, between concrete stalls and protective fences. Walking the long hall, one might lament the loss of the old soccer field, the sunlit strolls in the company of cows, the exotic parasols, or the crowd's giddy dashes to escape sudden downpours. Yet one still finds the familiar aisle of tomatoes raised into small pre-weighed piles, the tall pyramids of flour, the scent of saffron, the buzzing aisle of fish protected from the dust by a blanket of flies, and the fine jokes of the women vendors.

I meet Pio and Josiane, hand in hand. They laugh because they immediately sense my urge to pose still more questions about their marriage, to finally penetrate the mystery of the mutual promise they made each other in the marshes, a promise between a tall Tutsi cutter and a Hutu high school girl huddled beneath the papyrus, both of them pupils from the same class. Instead, we exchange the latest news. They tell me that the war Pio's mother has been waging against them—for she can't stand the idea of seeing her descendants contaminated by Tutsi blood—is now heading to court. At the end of their rope, they are leaving to the Mutara region, in the north of the country, to try their luck there.

The Mutara, an El Dorado of virgin prairies much discussed up on the hills, is the same region from which Jeannette returned at once utterly disillusioned and ruined. We find her farther on, in the tailors' row, hunched over her Singer. She recounts the dream she and her young husband shared of a sprawling parcel surmounted by wild pastures, the euphoria they felt as they embarked on their new adventure, taking their three children and the bundles in which they had wrapped the bounty from the sale of their land. Then the three hellish years in a windowless house, on arid land, the closest water supply at least two kilometers away, near a hamlet lacking both a school and a clinic.

And yet Jeannette had seen worse. In *Life Laid Bare*, she spoke of her mother's death as we talked in her small house in Kanazi. Then she added this: "I know for myself that when you've seen your mama cut so savagely and suffer so slowly, you forever lose a certain amount of trust in others, and not only in the *interahamwe*.* I mean, a person who has peered for so long into such terrible pain can never live among others like before. You are always wary. You distrust others even when they haven't done a thing. What I'm getting at is that Mama's death grieved me the most, but that her drawn-out suffering did me the most damage— and that can never be undone.'"

She was seventeen years old at the time, working the land to feed a family of orphaned children who had been brought together around her and her sister. Years later, during the drought of 2000, she gave up agriculture on a whim, tried her hand at business within a cooperative, took flight from her empty cashbox, and joined the local police force, from which she was expelled because of her slight build. Then she was given the gift of a sewing machine and married the father of her children, a pleasant young man, about whom she says: "His name is Sylvestre Bizimana. He's a bike-taxi driver. He brought me home in the evening several times after my sewing work at the market. We came to an understanding. Pregnancy followed. He showed affection . . . Now, debts come rolling in and money troubles pile up, but we have sorghum porridge aplenty . . . Heaven chose me to be a mother, and I gave birth—it's a big thing." The Bugesera air and her return to the tailors' shop have fortified her enthusiasm for her work, which isn't in short supply.

----

*Meaning "those who fight as a group," *interahamwe* refers to extremist Hutu militias created on the initiative of the Habyarimana clan, although it is impossible to gauge precisely the influence the clan exerted over them. They were trained by the Rwandan army, in some cases by French military advisers. The militias, whose active members numbered several tens of thousands, enlisted the hundreds of thousands of killers involved in the genocide. During the Tutsi-led RPF offensive in Congo in autumn 1996, many either dispersed or were killed, while others returned to Rwanda with the Hutu refugee population to turn themselves in.

A market day begins before the pink streaks of daybreak, when columns of people walk down from the dark hills surrounding Nyamata. The route sometimes takes more than four hours. Women carry sacks, baskets of beans, bound hens, bins filled with fruit, and sorghum—indeed everything the land has to offer. The lucky ones transport baskets of charcoal, the unlucky heavy sacks of flour. Rucksacks top off the load if no toddler is wrapped to the women's backs. Men push bicycles weighed down with more cumbersome sacks and sometimes with a goat, if it isn't trailing behind on a leash. They often tote bookbags containing the papers they plan to present at the clinic, the insurance office, or the district office. Because it is a market day, it is also the day for medical visits and administrative appointments.

Théophile carries nothing on his bike except, on the back-wheel rack, his beautiful wife, Francine, whose white shawl shields her from the dust, and atop the front bar, their daughter Aimée. He wears a herder's hat and carries a Tutsi staff. He drops the ladies at the market entrance, then pedals off contentedly to the first of several small cabarets, where he and other former breeders will swap stories about their herds. On the return trip, the men will bring the women home on their bicycles if their rounds of drinks haven't made them too wobbly to steer.

For some market-goers, the departure starts the night before instead of in the morning; cyclists transport their cargo of pineapples bound in nets from as far as Uganda, more than 150 kilometers away. From Kigali come moto-taxis loaded with secondhand clothes: jeans, shirts, and European-style dresses at cut-rate prices. The latter arouse less excitement than the mountain of ladies' shoes toward which the women gravitate, delighted. Eugénie loves sliding her feet into all kinds of pumps. She laughs as she takes a few steps in high heels. She says she was "a bit plump with plenty" after the birth of her seventh child. Francine picks out sandals for Aimée, who is taking school exams at the end of the week and could see herself in a pair of ballet flats. A shopkeeper sporting a broad-brimmed hat spreads out his tobacco leaves. Englebert comes here to smoke his pipe after bawdy chats with the merchant women.

Leaving at the other end of the covered market, we come upon bicycle mechanics and a scrapyard of machine parts and radio equipment. Deliverymen race past, their torsos shiny with sweat behind their wheelbarrows or their backs bent at right angles under sacks. The animal market resounds with restive groans, bleats, and cackles. Rabbits, newcomers to the Bugesera, are stupefied to find themselves rolled up like crepes at the bottom of baskets.

In the poultry section, we meet up with Immaculée as she selects a chicken for Sunday lunch. She likes to inspect their feet, to grope their hackles, then to play the crafty haggler as she wiggles in place. Immaculée is a teenager in perpetual motion. She bounds more than she walks; she jumps up and down as she talks. Everyone calls her Feza, her Rwandan name, except for me, who can't resist her Christian name, Immaculée. She delights in everything. Her curiosity is active from morning to night. She looks with smiling eyes on the world around her, giving the impression that her laughter and her gazelle-like skipping about stave off her timid nature.

IMMACULÉE FEZA

SIXTEEN YEARS OLD

Daughter of Innocent Rwililiza, Tutsi survivor

MY NAME IS IMMACULÉE FEZA AND I'M IN MY sixteenth year. There are four of us children in the family, two girls and two boys. I was born in a small house we call a *terre-tôle*, made of earth and sheet metal, in the run-down part of Gasenga. Then I grew up in the Kayumba neighborhood. Papa teaches at the high school. Mama works at the preschool and farms on our plot. Childhood has left me with happy memories. My family took great care of me. They gave me all they could, and they looked after my well-being in a way that spared me every cause of suffering. My mama took my hand on the walk to the little school; she saw me to church on Sundays. My papa showed me the straight and narrow. I was raised without any memorable hardship. We had endless fun between us sisters and brothers, and we enjoyed ourselves with the neighborhood kids, too. I hopped on one leg in hopscotch, I joined in ball games, and I danced. We were brought on trips to the Mutara to visit a maternal aunt, and a paternal aunt in Ntarama, and other family scattered across the district.

But I never spent my vacations with my parents' parents. They were cut by the machetes, all of them. I miss them very much. I often mourn their passing because they aren't here to encourage me. I know my childhood was a bit ruined by their absence. Yes, it really upsets me that I didn't get to meet them. Children who visit their grandparents come back in awe. They are sung incredible legends that their parents don't know. They discover illustrious characters known only to the elders.

In Africa, time refines our stories with the polish of magical words. The older the stories, the more they shine. Rwandan tales were missing from my childhood. It's frustrating. The killings harmed our sense of family. Without elders, wisdom slips away and family ceremonies come to be neglected. There is no one left to lecture us about how to behave at gatherings, to instill in us the kindness we owe the aged, or to scold us for shabby clothes. In Africa, families continually extend with each new brood of kids. Children make the rounds of their grandparents and granduncles and -aunts to be doted on from lap to lap. Grandparents rely on their grandchildren's young legs for the chores. They talk to each other without holding back. Sometimes children are scared to ask their parents questions; with the old folks, one feels freer to speak of personal things. It's something they enjoy. They know how to joke about how one's parents behave. But me, I have never had anyone to tell me how mine weaved their way through childhood. The elders might have told me about the killings differently. Like what? I don't know, maybe about a time when Tutsis and Hutus didn't interact like today, about their memories—that's what I have really missed out on.

I was eight years old when I learned the true story of the killings. Before that, I had only heard things mentioned on the radio or by my parents in the hush-hush of evening gatherings. They named the dead; it made them sad, as you'd expect. I heard them evoke lost family, people I didn't know. The killings hummed in our ears, but I didn't think much of it. They were words without a story, which pass children by. I didn't doubt what I heard, but

deep down the words weren't meant for me. My childhood continued carefree, because that's what life offered me.

Later, I was surprised by the extraordinary way people behaved during the Week of Mourning.* People screamed, they
sprinted aimlessly, they fell to their knees overflowing with tears.
Their gestures were frightening. I saw my mama crying one morning in the courtyard. Her silent sobs came pouring out, but as far
as we knew she wasn't hurt and hadn't had sad news. I got up the
courage to ask her. She spoke of her life in Kigali during the genocide with my sister, Ange. She told me about relatives who had
been cut. I visited the Nyamata memorial, the first time in her footsteps with my brothers and sister, a second time alone, trailing
Ange. I tuned in to the television shows and paid attention to the
civics lessons. Afterward, when I felt comfortable enough, I dug
up hidden information on the internet.

The genocide is familiar to me now. I know a lot about how
my parents lived, and there is always more I want to know. Papa
ran through the Kayumba forest. He bolted down the slopes like
so many others. They lay flat in the ditches, thorns stuck in their
bare feet. They threw themselves in the thickets to stay alive. Each
morning, the ones who woke without illness did their best to hold
out until dark. During the night, they ate bananas and raw cassava;
they drank water from the rainy season. I've pieced together the
details. Fugitives by the thousands went up to the forest, and
twenty were chosen to come back down with their lives. The good
Lord saved Papa. It wasn't the extraordinary strength of his legs

---

*April 7, a national holiday since 1995, marks the beginning of a week of national
mourning, which includes presidential speeches, processions, radio and television
programs, and local ceremonies, in particular at memorial sites. Certain regions post-
pone the commemorations because of specific events; in Butare, for example, they begin on April 19, and in Bisesero, on June 27.

or his brave heart. I know it was his fate to be guided by the dear Lord through all the zigzags of his escape.

Papa is good at telling the story, like a sad fairy tale—Mama, too, though she doesn't play the teacher as much. She speaks softly. When they recount their experiences, they use a calm voice and hide their feelings from their children's eyes. It upsets me to know how they lived—lower than animals. It doesn't make me ashamed. I imagine my mama hidden in a ceiling the whole day, and my papa almost naked, exhausting himself in his breathless sprints. These thoughts pierce me with dread. Have I visited my mama's hiding place in Kigali? No, there's been no opportunity to. I went up to the Kayumba forest with schoolmates. We had heard the accounts of survivors running for their lives. We were anxious to see the huge forest for ourselves. We walked through the thorny under-growth and the little gullies on the trail of their memories. Fate hounded my parents—it wanted them dead beneath the machete blades. They survived hostile forces, they escaped evil. I'm proud of such beautiful parents.

THIS IS MY second year at Nyamata Catholic, the secondary school next to the church. It's a coed school, which my parents chose. We study in peace. The subjects I like best: biology and geography. I am neither the smartest in class nor lagging behind. It's good. For sports: volleyball.

I get up at 5:30. After heartfelt prayers, I do the dishes, I wash up, then I'm off to school. At seven o'clock, we have assembly, and classes begin at 7:30. Lessons last fifty minutes, recesses fifteen. At 2:30, I come home. I eat, then I clean the family clothes, and at six o'clock begin the evening's schoolwork. At suppertime, the family gathers for the meal. We used to eat mostly beans, but now there are different vegetables because of my papa's health. After the meal, we share news and swap jokes between us brothers and sisters. Our parents sometimes encourage us to stop and think about things. Sleep overtakes me very quickly.

I'm up at six on the weekends. I get the porridge ready, I scrub the wash, I give Mama a hand with the cooking. I like to think I'm good at preparing food—I brown the plantains in oil or the sweet potatoes. Papa's illness means no beans. Housework I like. Everything except for cleaning the kitchen utensils, fetching water, and, of course, farming. In the afternoons, I leave to meet my girlfriends. We don't have any particular places. Most of the time we sit by the hedgerows, we talk without forethought or study schoolwork in the yard. We sometimes stroll down to Nyamata's main street, but we don't go to the cabaret or to the cinema, either, because there isn't one. We lack the money for outside entertainment, and getting our parents' permission is a problem. We haven't yet learned to disobey. We're happy enough hanging out on the street. We say hello to friends we happen to meet, and we share whatever comes to mind.

If we drop in at the Cultural Center, it's during rec times. Dancing makes me happier than anything. I love to dance surrounded by friends. I lose myself laughing. We also go to watch movies or music videos, especially Rwandan or American music, and the Rwandan team's soccer games. I'm fond of war movies with uplifting endings. Nigerian soaps are a delight because the actors have very fancy manners—they are more attractive than American actors and all the rest. I tag along with my brother Valois to a cybercafé on the main street. We browse the news and keep an eye on world events, of course. We watch the performers, the dancers and singers, on YouTube. We chat with friends on Facebook. We explore amazing websites. Valois shows them to me because he has them at his fingertips. They describe the world's catastrophes and explain the evil rites used by secret societies to stir up wars. They talk about the punishments in store for mankind in the afterlife, the dark forces taking over the universe, defiling it more thoroughly than all the massacres one can imagine—sort of the warning signs of the apocalypse. We aren't the only ones to visit these wicked sites—almost all young people do. At some point, we simply won't be able to stay away; it's a world that excites our imagination. We also visit funny sites to laugh at the jokes.

My greatest joy is running off to the market, which is always a big temptation because it lets me escape the boredom at home. I can't even find the words to describe how exhilarating it is, probably because being around all those people never gets old. It's so much fun to hear and see so many things. I know how to bargain for the best prices, and I make my counteroffers firm, despite my young age. At the market, one runs into friends from other schools who come to buy things or just wander around, and we swap jokes more than actual news.

AT SCHOOL, a group of friends and I often discuss the genocide. It can come up anytime, during recess, for example, often on our way to places, far from other people's ears. Someone might mention it after a history lesson or want to work through new details heard on a radio show. Sometimes an incident occurs in one of our families and the person needs to talk to relieve their anxiety. This is more frequent during the Week of Mourning, when trauma erupts everywhere. You see students at school who go off by themselves to sulk, some with their heads down on their desks, and who won't utter a word the whole day. Some are thrown into a tumult and thrash about violently. For example, students start running and screaming about machetes. They scream that someone is coming to cut them or that they have already been cut. When a student behaves like that, the principal steps in straightaway to have him taken to the clinic. He calls on the student's friends to gather around to comfort him. Later, classmates come together and we share what we're feeling. Some of us are shaken up; others are used to it. We split into small groups, then, to talk about what happened. There are cases of troubled kids insulting Hutus. They distrust Hutu faces and they shout mean words. Their friends show sympathy. Others are indifferent or embarrassed— they don't know what feelings to express.

Yes, there are brawls occasionally. When students hurl insults, sometimes fists fly. For example, students might provoke a boy by harping on his parent's misdeeds. Or the opposite, they deliberately go past a person, making believe that they don't know what week it is, that nothing important ever happened anyway, or that they couldn't care less about all the fuss. Behavior like that riles people up. We also had a girl once who wrote her schoolmates threatening messages: "You've done so much killing that now you're going to pay for it. We've got our eyes on you." On the other side, a boy student wrote anonymous notes saying, "We killed your family, but it's not enough. We're going to finish the job." Three times he left the same notes on desks during recess. The principal marched off to the police, but they never discovered who it was. Most of the time, students choose avoidance.

I steer clear of ethnic arguments. I keep from discussing the genocide with my Hutu classmates. Not one of them has ever come up to me and suggested talking about it. I think they are too uncomfortable. With my good Tutsi girlfriends, we can discuss our parents' troubles—their quirks, so to speak. It doesn't happen often. For example, certain parents break down right in the middle of the day; as soon as someone mentions the killings, they become agitated or morose. Friends have run away from home because of their parents' behavior. A classmate told me that her mama abandoned them to escape the poverty brought about by the genocide.

Several classmates say that they feel really worn down by the mess at home: the drinking, their parents' eccentricities and neglect. I know some who try to find peace and quiet with their distant relatives.

Hutu children don't talk about these things as much. They talk very little. To hear them tell it, there's nothing out of the ordinary at home. They reject the chance to be consoled. They never reveal what their family lives are like. Plenty of young Hutus pretend they don't know what their parents did. There are some who repeat how sick they are of always hearing about the genocide; some seem ashamed, and others are bitter—they praise their parents' courage. I'm young: when in doubt, I avoid discussions with them.

I PRAY WITH all my heart every morning. I say a special prayer for the safety of the country so that my loved ones no longer tremble, and I ask for extra help when difficulties arise at home. My mama drew me to religion, but I'm the one who chose the Presbyterian church, because it's near our house. My faith runs deep. I believe that a people's destruction is the will of God. He decided who should die and who should be saved. Why would a benevolent God, with infinite goodness and supreme power, accept the almost total extermination of the Tutsis by their neighbors? That's a good question. I don't know the answer. I don't understand any of God's reasons, except that He may have wanted to demonstrate His omnipotence, because now the survivors can bear witness to it. I am too young a girl to grasp the depths of theology. The dark soul of mankind holds temptations; maybe God puts people to the test. I don't know.

God is a mystery; I'm in favor of that idea. The mystery doesn't alter my faith in the least. Still, I know people whose faith has faded. They have abandoned the church or are so unsure that you barely see them from one Sunday to the next. The sermons no longer flow through them; they have stopped closing their eyes to drink in the pastor's words. Certain others are constantly changing parishes. The whole family goes to the Catholics and they come away disappointed; then they turn to the Adventists, they last a month, and off they go, following a colleague someplace else.

They flee their uncertainty. I don't at all share their doubts, but I understand their tendency to let everything drop. Myself, I don't pray to erase the present or the past. My faith doesn't relieve the sorrow that my thoughts of lost family cause. No, no, that much I'm sure I know. My faith doesn't make me more trusting toward people. In my view, it gives human beings more strength. It protects me, anyway.

FISHING ON THE AKAGERA

IN THE MIDDLE OF THE NIGHT, AS THE COALS IN the courtyard go out, Idelphonse leaves home, fishnets over his shoulder. He crosses the center of Kiganwa, exchanging a few words with the silhouettes chatting in the glow of the candlelight on the verandas. He follows a stretch of path, then turns down a trail that descends abruptly toward the river. In the darkness of the banana groves, the coos of turtledoves answer the cuckoos' calls, their odes interrupted by the barks of what may be jackals or monkeys.

Down the hill, lapping water lets one know the river is near. In the shadows, its current seems stock-still. The water is slack; even during the rainy season, it barely stirs. On clear nights, the moon and even the stars are reflected on its surface. A tongue of earth skirts the river, surrounded by sloping pastures. A dozen years ago, these banks held the barrel-like shadows of hippos. Herds grazed until daybreak. The females mooed at their cavorting calves while the males grunted, marking their territory for the umpteenth time with mounds of droppings. Today the fishermen lament the animals' absence because, they say, the squat pachyderm hooves used to mill the mud, working into the current the plankton and insects the fish were fond of. Nowadays, only cow dung mixes with the sludge. The cows come at night to graze on the aquatic fodder, which young kids, night owls balanced atop thin boats, cut into islets for them to eat along the riverside. Yet the hippos didn't leave because of the cows, and still less because of the gaggle of geese one sees coiled in the grass at the edge of the bush. It was the sugarcane planters. Indeed, the green-gold fever of Kigali's investors has spread all the way here.

As Idelphonse inspects his traps, other fishermen arrive and deposit their gear into slender pirogues. They silently slide their boats into the river and depart for deeper waters, baiting their hooks with beeswax before setting up their traps and lines in the choppy current. In the morning, the fishermen return home singing, just as people in pirogues sing nearly everywhere in the world. A hustle and bustle awaits them on the banks. Women do their wash kneeling at the water's edge; herders goad their cattle to drink. A bevy of herons, touching down from who knows where, scour the rushes with their hungry beaks. During the migration season, egrets bivouac here as well. The heat has stopped the gray geese from sleeping in; they graze the grass unperturbed by the commotion around them.

The fishermen empty their catch onto the landing. Tilapia are tossed into a red bucket, barbs into a green one, small catfish into pails carried off by female fish-merchants to be smoked and then sold at the market. Idelphonse can't hide his disappointment. It was a luckless morning with the nets. An eel or a plump Nile perch could have earned him and his colleagues several thousand francs from Kigali restaurants.

When he returns from the river, he walks past the parcel where his mother and brother, Jean-Damascène, are busy tilling the soil. Scarcely a word is said between them. For Idelphonse, the workday is over. He goes for a stroll with friends from the fishing co-op until mealtime and then takes a nap. Afterward, he sees to the *urwagwa*, whose secret recipe his father, during his years of freedom, handed down to him.* The banana beer Idelphonse distills delights his Kiganwa customers, who sit on the veranda passing around the *chalumeau* late into the evening, some admirers coming from as far as Nyarunazi or Kibungo for its exceptional taste.†

Unlike his brother, Idelphonse hardly thrived at school. Leaving was less of a disappointment than he lets on. He didn't dream of a job in town. He pictured himself instead alongside his father, Fulgence, who trained him in business and in new crops like tomatoes and coffee. He learned fast. A tenacious worker, he spared no effort to succeed. He had been looking forward to a good marriage on the hill, a house in Kiganwa, and later a business of his own, until the day the Ernestine Kaneza affair changed everything. It was a Sunday, sixteen years after the genocide. During the final session of the *gaçaça* trials, to everyone's surprise, Janvier Munyaneza's story of the horrid murder of his sister Ernestine, on the first day of the killings, sent Idelphonse's father back to Rilima for life. On that notorious Sunday night, as Idelphonse followed the three men leading Fulgence away in shackles, he still didn't know the reason for his father's arrest, for no one in his family had attended the trial. He thought it merely a momentary twist of fate, which would explain his shock the next day when he discovered the details.

At nineteen years old, he is no longer the little boy who watched his father leave for prison after their return from Congo.

Urwagwa, or banana beer, is four times less expensive and three times stronger than ordinary beer; it can also be quite delicious—hence its popularity on the hills. It varies in tartness depending on the brewer's expertise and may even be sweet to suit the drinker's taste. Hutus are said to be more skilled at brewing *urwagwa* than Tutsis, although that doesn't make them any more fervent devotees.

†*Chalumeau* is the reed straw placed in a bottle of *urwagwa*. Cabaret regulars buy a bottle at a time and pass it around to their companions.

At that time, at least one man from every Hutu family in Kiganwa was in prison. The children shared the same incomprehension, destitution, and humiliation. This time, however, the family had to confront alone the rumors and shame brought on by the accusations of the appalling crime. They kept their feelings of injustice to themselves. Their hopes for an appeal dwindled; the signs of their poverty quickly appeared. The parents of Idelphonse's fiancée refused to accept him as their son-in-law, his brother was expelled from school, their crops declined in Fulgence's absence. There were endless arguments in the fields, which their neighbors eyed covetously. Idelphonse gradually gave up the hoe, preferring his nights spent fishing on the silent river. He rarely mentions his troubles. He goes on walks; he drinks in Primus the money he makes from fishing, which he then earns back by selling *urwagwa*.

IDELPHONSE HABINSHUTI

NINETEEN YEARS OLD

Son of Fulgence Bunani, Hutu prisoner

WHEN I FISH, I'M OUT THE DOOR IN THE EVENING.
With farming, I'm up at five o'clock. It's a little over a two-kilometer walk to the field. Mama joins me after housework around the yard. Our plot takes up some seven and a half acres in a place called Batsinda, near the river. When Papa's strength set the pace for ours, the land gave in abundance. It yields plenty to those who put a lot of effort into it. I take a break once the sun begins beating down. I head home for lunch, rest while the sun lasts, and return to the field until 5:30 or 6:00. I get washed, I relax. If I scrape up enough, I buy myself a Primus, because it's a treat. Otherwise, I have some *urwagwa* or sorghum porridge—that's good, too. Our family makes them tasty.

Since Papa's imprisonment, it's been up to me to distill the bananas for the *urwagwa*. How? You select bunches of slightly bitter bananas, you add plantains, and you bury them four days. You take them out and mash them in a bucket with herbs. You grill the sorghum, you mix it with the juice for the fermentation, and you bury it again to contain the fumes. After a day's wait, you pull out the tasty *urwagwa* that everyone craves. In our family, I don't make decisions in place of my papa, because I was born a child with only my mama in front of me. But in the drink business, it's me who speaks up and she who takes my side.

In the evenings, I go for walks around Nyarunazi, see pals, or get a shave. I'm asleep at nine o'clock unless a friend stops in to chat. Nothing but rest on Sundays. I'm a good Catholic but not so fervent. I pray for Papa before bed. I appeal to God again when I get up. One still wonders, though, how a good and all-powerful God could shut His eyes to such killings. I gladly attend mass but not every Sunday. Afterward, I stroll around Kibungo or else I wash clothes. I visit friends—I join them in their courtyards, or we meet along the way to shoot the breeze. We share our thoughts and bottles of beer.

There are no televisions in Kiganwa. In Nyamata, I don't stay to watch; I couldn't name my favorite programs. You won't find a field for kicking the ball around, either, because farming has swallowed up all the flat plots of land. I listen to the Rwandan team's matches on the radio. I root for all the national team's players, Michel Ndahinduka in particular—he's a dribbler from Nyamata. In his childhood he wore our jersey with the striker's number nine. A friend owns a smartphone. We watch movies, but I'm not overeager to see how they end. We listen to music videos. Rwandan music makes me happy, of course, and the music of young people my age like Tom Close or Kitoko, especially dance music. Do I dance? Not enough time. And where would I? Every month I head to the Nyamata market to sell sweet potatoes, or cassava flour, or beans when prices bottom out. I take advantage of the trip to buy an outfit or a phone card and cheer on the Nyamata team with the others around the soccer field. Go to a cabaret? Never, I haven't got the money. Listen to a band some night at the Black and White? I haven't got polished shoes. When I visit the family in Kigali, we stroll the streets, we admire the new neighborhoods, and we share news about relatives we haven't seen for a time. My cousins point out where prestigious people live. We obviously don't go in anywhere; I've never stepped foot in a movie theater or an internet café. Anyway, I don't know how to work the computer.

MY NAME MEANS "one always counts on friends." My father's the one who chose it. I was born in 1992, I don't know the month. There are four of us children in the family. My father is called Fulgence Bunani. He lives in Rilima. He was first put in prison after we returned from Congo. Our country's president pardoned him in the seventh year of his sentence. In 2010, a *gaçaça* trial sent him back again. We were disappointed beyond measure. Before that, he had proved himself a praiseworthy farmer, his business prospered, and the *urwagwa* trade filled his pockets.

My mama's name is Jacqueline Mukamana. As a farmer, she holds her own on the family plot; she carries on quite capably with my papa away. I have stood by her on the parcel from the age of seventeen; basically, since my papa's return to prison. I fish at night on the Akagera River. I didn't leave school gladly. The first time I was expelled; I was in my third year of primary school—I was fifteen. I had a clever hand at math, and I saw myself in a premium job later on. But the principal called Mama in, demanding the *minervals* right there and then. She lowered her gaze. He warned her that with each payment we missed, he would send me home. Poverty led to more comings and goings; Mama could see that she was stuck. The land refused to give her good harvests. She handed me the hoe and asked me to be patient on the parcel.

In 2003, Papa was released with a long line of repentant prisoners. Once home, he took the hoe from my hands. The parcel produced in abundance, and the harvest paid the *minervals*. For two years, I returned to school, until the first semester of my fifth year. I had my sights set on studying crafts so I could learn a trade in town. Then my papa was taken back to prison in 2010. That was the end of school. At the penitentiary, he offered to sell a strip of land to cover tuition, but Mama decided that I would stay on in farming. I was a little angry. Not too much, though, since I knew that selling land would set off a family feud.

I FIRST HEARD about the war when we were in Congo. I was a little boy. We lived two years in the Masisi camp, next to the volcano. My papa distilled and sold his drink, my mama sold her strength in the Congolese women's fields. I went with her because preschool was rare. I don't remember any tough times in Congo. It was good for a child; we children played. Except at the end, when everyone was mistreated. The soldiers fired their artillery shells, and it was an awful tumult of bloody panic and fear. We left the camp sprinting; we trekked in columns for days to Gisenyi. Trucks transported us to the district, where we walked to our hill in Kiganwa. The house stood in a sorry state, with no sheet metal on the roof and broken windows. Scrub was eating away the land. Papa didn't last more than two weeks at home. The soldiers came, tied his arms, and took him away to the penitentiary with his colleagues from the hill.

Mama went down alone to clear the plot of brush. She started planting what to eat. The Tutsi neighbors glared at us, of course, and many hurled threats. The way to school could be full of dread. It was risking shame to get too close to a prisoner's kid. It wasn't easy going to Nyarunazi or Kibungo. We dodged stones as well as insults. When trouble lurked, we walked behind the bushes, following in each other's steps. Sometimes, when we couldn't avoid going through the center of Nyarunazi, survivors pitted children against each other. Their words made war between us. I had to put up with it—I couldn't very well change papas.

When neighbors talked about Congo at evening gatherings, the little one that I was perked up his ears. I might even ask them for details. If the questions seemed valid, and not too demanding, the neighbors offered answers. This was in the evening. Later, in the black of night, my childish imagination would lead me back to the commotion of the camp and frighten me in the midst of machetes with a dance of threatening faces. It all happened in another world. Then I waited for the faces to return from where they'd come.

Like any child deprived of his papa, I wanted to know why mine wasn't coming home. Mama said a few words about the killings, but she didn't explain my papa's captivity. I listened carefully to the rumors. The first thing I heard was that a lot of people had been cut in Ntarama, in Kibungo, and everywhere else. I followed the radio programs. I listened to tearful music and commentaries. I went with a cousin to visit the memorial.

The marshes, though, never. I don't have a single colleague whom I'd dare suggest it to. I haven't had the opportunity to go with someone meticulous with the facts. I lack a decent education to talk about the genocide openly with friends. In Kiganwa, we barely mention it; we don't have the curiosity or the time. We make passing remarks about what we hear on the radio, and rumors are all one gets from casual conversations, at the cabaret, or on the way to work. But families share nothing of their private thoughts. At school, they teach the extermination. The lessons are meant to be general, emptied of accusations. Among Tutsi schoolmates, though, there's no hide-and-seek. They attack you if you set about talking like that.

The truth has found its place as I've left childhood behind.

Now I'm familiar with the history I hear during the commemorations. But as I said, it's different with explanations in the family. I've questioned Mama about Papa. She said that he's the only one who can provide satisfactory answers about the genocide. She refuses to answer in his place. She's a loyal wife. She's not spendthrift or blameworthy. She fears the traditional anger a husband feels when confronted with a bad wife; she refuses to make his imprisonment worse. She never gets angry with him.

In Rilima, Papa received a sentence of twelve years; he stayed for seven. I don't know if the punishment makes up for his misdeeds. How could I know? When he left in 2003, he didn't explain things directly; he didn't address his wrongdoing. He told us that he had acknowledged sins of genocide at his trial, that he had received a pardon in return. Sometimes he told us about his prisoner routine, about his duties and chores, how he and his colleagues had gotten through those years in prison. Then he described the miracle of his release.

Still, he never sat me down on a bench in the yard to share his opinion of the killings with me. He returned to running the parcel and the cabaret without bothering about explanations. He showed himself to be a remarkable farmer again. The house's veranda, he built that. He planted a banana grove, he distilled his renowned *urwagwa*. It's impossible to figure out the thoughts of a father after he has spent seven years in prison. Before the killings, people said he was very devout. He read from the Bible wearing the deacon's robe, and he preached as the priest's replacement at less important masses. After he was freed, he didn't miss church a single Sunday. But it's hard to know now if he prays with any fervor.

I felt some frustration, of course. It's complicated having a papa who has just left prison. Shortly after that, in 2010, I went to sit in the grass at the *gaçaça* courts. I listened to the trials without flinching. We heard a lot of unexpected information. One acquaintance would accuse another, "You were in an expedition that Sunday. I saw you in the marshes below Nyarunazi." Or, "You're the one who struck my sister with your machete. Everyone saw you." The witnesses' accounts poured out. People accused the criminals; we learned who had done wrong on which day in which place. I heard my papa answer questions and listened to him describe several of his expeditions. It was agonizing.

When the trials ended, I was wary of learning more. I only wanted to hear the facts from my papa's lips. I'm not sure now—it's a bit confused. Maybe I just wasn't curious anymore. A child doesn't want to hear everything his papa has to say. In any case, on the last day of the *gaçaça*, they gave him a life sentence because of the business with Ernestine and her baby boy. They tied him up and took him to Rilima right there and then.

A PILE OF CASSAVA

WITH KEEN PRECISION, HER HAND DRIVES THE blade into the cassava bulb, picks the bulb up with the blade, and drops it in her other hand to strip the cassava bare in a few quick cuts. Two last chops lop off the ends, and the fat root is tossed atop the pile. In Claudine's hand the machete whirls in an unbroken rhythm even as she chats with a visitor or lectures a child on the other side of the hedge. One senses that her skill runs in the family, a dexterity handed down from her mother or grandmother before their deaths. Her legs outstretched, her back set against a low stone wall, she sits on a cloth facing two pyramidal piles. The entire season's harvest will pass beneath her blade—between the shrinking pile of brown cassava and the rising pile of peeled, white bulbs—before being hauled off to the mill.

Claudine speaks in her distinctive low voice. She poses questions about Parisian life, the height of the buildings, the climate in France. She asks for news about my mama and her health, and she wonders about my siblings' work. She is curious about all the traveling that journalists do. Don't they get tired of gathering such chaotic news? How do they eat so far from home? Do they find wives in every country? She is also one of the few people who inquire about my books.

Her foot is giving her trouble; its arch looks dreadfully swollen. The exams she had at the hospital in Kigali failed to reveal anything conclusive enough for the doctors to diagnose the ailment. The healer near Ntarama, whom she has consulted since childhood, attempted several remedies before confessing her bewilderment. "It's the poison of jealousy," says Claudine. "There's no shortage of it around here."

The construction site behind her may very well be the cause of the jealousy. On the spot of her old adobe dwelling, still the standard in the *mudugudu*, rise the roughcast-cement walls of a home like those now found in Nyamata. The windows await windowpanes; the house frame stands ready to support a V-shaped roof and a ceiling for insulation. She and her husband, Damascène Bizima, had a stroke of luck when the new asphalt road leading to the future airport in Kigali arrived alongside their property, a strip of which Damascène sold to developers at a premium price. The couple is also building a hut for a *mudugudu* grocery in a corner of their yard and, at the opposite end, a pen for their cow as well as the goats that will soon be joining them. As Claudine remarks, "Good fortune was passing on the road and made a stop for us."

We are waiting for Nadine. Damascène was hostile to our initial interview three days earlier, a position he justified by relating his fear that the narrative of certain episodes from Nadine's life might prove harmful to the entire family. More than he lets on at first, he has plainly been stung by the mockery to which they have been subjected in recent years. This explains why he had put Nadine on her guard, although he did so to such an extent that she said almost nothing during our first conversation. Fortunately, Claudine intervened. She doesn't share Damascène's anxiety, doubtless thanks to her past experience with my books; she knows that a story published in France has no effect on the rumors here. She also no doubt believes that her daughter, by telling her story to a sympathetic stranger, may be able to express what she tends to fixate on in silence, that talking to me will encourage Nadine to open up about "her roots," which, as Claudine puts it, "got tangled up in sorrow." In convincing her husband to allow us to speak one-on-one, Claudine displayed both diplomacy and a touch of guile. Most important, she put her daughter's mind at ease.

Nadine finally arrives. She has donned a cherry-red sheath dress and matching turban for the occasion. She pauses a moment, hesitating in the doorway. We give her a round of applause. She turns in place, kisses her mother, who leaves the room with Damascène, and settles comfortably in an armchair. She was four years old in the photograph published in *Life Laid Bare*. Because she spoke neither English nor French, I saw her grow up over the years without really speaking to her. She is now the eldest child of a lovely family. With an air of nonchalance and a mischievous smile, she knows that she is a beautiful girl whose curves hold the gaze of the boys from the *mudugudu* as well as those from her class. But what is most striking is how similar her deep voice is to her mother's.

NADINE UMUTESI

SEVENTEEN YEARS OLD

Daughter of Claudine Kayitesi, Tutsi survivor

THIS RED DRESS I'M WEARING, I CHOSE IT MYSELF. My mama took me to the boutique called Mama Codé, where the lady showed off all the dresses to us. It was a big thing. I picked the red one, Mama approved, and afterward Papa admired my choice. We all had a bit of fun. Sometimes people tease me that I am a beautiful girl. That makes me happy. It's a good sign. Can being pleasing bring me luck? I think so, anyway.

My name is Nadine Umutesi; I don't know what it means. I am seventeen years old, the oldest child, with three brothers, and no sister for the moment. As a little girl, I lived with my mama, Claudine, just the two of us. She would bring me with her to our field, and while she raised the hoe I would entertain myself on a mat spread out in the shadow of a tree. When I was older, I played with the other children brought to the fields like me. I remember Berthe and her children. Together we formed a family where no male voice could be heard. Later on, Mama married Papa. He showed himself to be kind, like a papa, and we loved each other like a family. My childhood went by happily because I wasn't clever enough yet to understand that pitfalls were lurking around me.

My papa's name is Damascène; he works at the Ntarama
Health Center. My mama farms our plot of land beside the asphalt
road. I don't know where I was born. It was in Congo, anyway, in
the Masisi region, where, people tell me, the famous Karisimbi volcano rumbles. That's where my mama was dragged off to. When
she returned from Congo, I lived my youngest years near the
Kanzenze bus stop, in the adobe house at the top of the way—you
know, where your friend took the photos. In 2003, we left to live
here in the *mudugudu*, which put us closer to our plot. That's a
good thing, although it is farther from where I go to school, at
Nelson Mandela. I am in my second year of secondary school.

IT ALL STARTED in primary school. When the teachers
would ask for my father's name, I would answer, Damascène
Bizima. There was one teacher who contradicted me in front of
the class; he claimed that I was a liar. Then a second one. The
two of them said he wasn't my real papa. They were show-offs,
of course, who wanted to be mean. They enjoyed making the
students laugh and bringing chaos to our family. Among us, it's a
custom to intimidate the unlucky ones.

I put up with the taunts because there were no worries, no
danger at home. I didn't notice anything abnormal in my parents.
They got on well, and they seemed happy with their daughter. I
was looked after with loving care. Then one day, an ill-boding
neighbor stopped me at our gate. He told me why my papa wasn't
the real one. It was an extraordinary surprise. I had always looked
on Damascène as my papa regardless of the rumors. I was very
confused.

I mustered the courage to ask my mother for the truth. In her
sweetest voice, she spoke into my eyes. She told me that during the
genocide, women were sometimes made pregnant by savage men.

She herself was violated by an *interahamwe* who forced her to follow him all the way to Congo. He made her his servant. That's how I was born. Ever since I found out, I feel caught in a kind of uneasiness; I feel trapped by a sense of something like disgust. But I accepted the news as it was, because Papa continued to provide me with a papa's love, as if he hadn't heard a thing. I kept my composure, and I continue to see him as my true papa.

Before the revelation, I was already aware of the genocide through radio programs. It was during the Week of Mourning. The neighbors discussed it, especially the ones getting on in age. They recalled what had happened to them. I heard how Tutsis had been cut by Hutus. They were so racked with hunger that they ate raw cassava even though they knew it was bad for their stomach. A lady described how she became so bloated from eating it that she couldn't move from under the papyrus for three days. They prayed for rain to fall hard and fast because then the killers would ignore them and turn instead to looting houses—especially the sheet metal roofs they were so greedy for. The neighbors would share their memories once a year, which isn't so much.

The genocide was something we avoided at home, except maybe when my back was turned. In class, there were no quarrels between kids. I was too naive to understand completely. I didn't suspect a thing. It was after the revelation that I asked to be told. One night the family was together—Papa, Mama, and I—and Mama explained the killings and everything that happened in detail. I was twelve years old. She revealed what she had seen personally; she described her mama sliced with a machete. They numbered seven in her family; two of them survived. I don't know much about my lost uncles and aunts.

Above all, Claudine offered me her memories of my grandmother. She seemed a kindly woman, and Claudine and the other children loved her dearly. She was never mean; she looked upon her offspring and neighbors with caring eyes. She knew fairy tales, and she pushed her children in school despite the poverty they endured. In Damascène's family, his papa and mama were cut in Kanzenze. His whole family died around there. I don't know how—I'm not sure of the details because the family was so large.

I have peered far into the darkness of the genocide. I have continued to ask question after question either about Claudine or about her family. About the origin of the killings, about how people hid in the papyrus before the sun came out, how they crept through the water surrounded by mosquitoes, eating raw food when they gathered at night, and how they managed to survive while most others were cut. I have been to the Ntarama memorial, although I am not at all interested in going into the marshes. Basically, I don't want to know things that are too tangible. Eating with muddy hands, sleeping in filth, living in clothes torn off by thorns—all of that upsets me. I am keener to learn about Congo because the criminals brought my mama there. I crave specifics. I look forward to taking a trip to Congo later on. I would like to examine the landscape of the place where I took my first breath. That's understandable, right?

My papa gives his full support to what my mama says, but she alone explains the genocide. When she talks, I don't see any trouble on her face. I think she conceals it. She speaks in her beautiful voice, which you know because you ask her so many questions you jot down in your notebooks. She sidesteps the everyday details of life in Congo, but otherwise she speaks without zigzags. When she's vague in a description, I ask her to clarify. I avoid interrupting her with questions that might make her suffer. I know she has been hurt. Hearing the truth seems less essential than stifling certain dreadful secrets. It helps me adjust to the obstacles in my life.

. . .

I GET UP at six o'clock, I wash, and I go down to the roadside. If no kindhearted driver gives me a lift to the bus stop, I call a bike-taxi on my mobile, which is a three-hundred-franc ride. I'm back home at 3:30 in the afternoon.

I enjoy myself at school, even if we don't have anything to eat for lunch. I get grades that bode well for my passing the national exam later on. I am refining my skills on the computer—my school has fourteen of them. We learn word processing, we listen to music, we check out websites, we try to find incredible stories to surprise ourselves with. Myself, I steer clear of the worst of them. I look at Facebook, although not very much. In class, you can be punished for it. I have to use a friend's smartphone to open my page. I play soccer on a really excellent team, with practices three times a week. On defense is where I earn the accolades. The number five jersey brings out my best—or the number six, in the midfield, when the coaches ask me to, because I can handle the running and love to launch attacks like the Dutch. I see friends on the field and we find times to chitchat.

Once back home, I eat immediately. There's no noon lunch, as I said. Afterward, I prepare the evening food and study for school. I see my close friends before the evening meal. We talk a lot, we joke and tease each other; laughing like girls never gets old. Sometimes we share class notes and homework. I nod off at nine o'clock. On the weekends, I prepare the morning tea and do the housecleaning. Afterward, it's up to me to make the noon and evening meals alongside Mama. I don't work on the parcel, not even spading. I lend a hand with weeding only after unexpected rains. Claudine keeps me from the fatigue of farming. She insists that I not spoil my strength in the field. Only when the cowherd is away will I mind a cow and its calf with a staff in the pastures, or sometimes I bring grass to the cowshed. It isn't very far.

I don't know a thing about movies. I haven't been to the cinema. Where would I go? In Kanzenze there is no movie theater, and in Nyamata there are only films with kung fu fights and the like. When I travel to Kigali for vacations, I visit an aunt but we never go to places that charge admission. Neighbors invite me to watch television, especially during vacations. We applaud the petty lovers' squabbles just like at the theater. My very favorite thing is the Rwandan national team's games.

I have a sweetheart. We get along well. We take long aimless walks. We don't go down to Nyamata very often because getting our parents' permission is complicated. I'm waiting for my twentieth birthday before I disobey. I know how to dance until I'm so exhausted my head spins. Dancing is my passion. In the school's troupe we dance to traditional folk songs. The dance is called *umushagiriro*; we set the tempo by stamping our feet on the ground. At church we dance to Negro spirituals, in ecstasy, so to speak. It's a blast. I sing and dance very prettily. People admire me, and I am always in demand.

I was fifteen years old when I became very religious. I feel so good at church. I go on Monday and Wednesday evenings and Saturdays and Sundays during the day. We sing and we pray. I share in the cleaning duties, I dance. It makes me happy to go to church. Although my parents are religious, I don't go to please them. Our neighbors influenced our choice of parish. I devote myself to prayer and meet a lot of acquaintances there.

I have friends from both ethnicities, of course. At church, it's essential, and at school, too. I don't ever discuss the genocide with young people from the other ethnicity. I talk about different things, not about that. Reticence wins out. I think that young people are often upset by what they hear in their families or by the films they see. And there are sometimes run-ins at school. An orphan might get angry and say something nasty to a Hutu schoolmate, for example: "Get lost, we've got no use for you anymore." The Hutu child complains, says he's insulted, and won't let it go. Everyone gathers around, tempers flare, and soon they're grabbing at each other's collars.

That's less common than it used to be. Now the girls tend to be more aggressive than the boys when the killings come up. They don't step aside; they strike with their words. I'm not sure why. Maybe they see themselves as more vulnerable, so they are quicker to vent what they feel deep down inside. The safest thing is to keep out of it. I am wary of the turmoil and trauma that arise in groups of young people; the yelling frightens me. I prefer not to get involved. In Hutu families they talk about things in their own way, although I couldn't say how exactly, because I don't know young Hutus' thoughts. I don't get close to their innermost feelings.

I have a friend I confide in when my heart is heavy. She is a close friend I share the walk to school with. Her name is Olive. She is the same age as me and lives in the lane overlooking our *mudugudu*. We are in the same situation: she, too, was born of a brutal seed. She came to tell me herself when she heard the rumors about me. It was a natural conversation, so to speak. We often talk over things because we understand each other. We both crave more distractions. We would love to listen to music with other young people in Nyamata. It would cheer us up. The only chances for amusement in Kanzenze are the soccer ball and traditional dance. My mama and I have discussed it, so now she tolerates my going out more often.

I SOMETIMES THINK about the papa who gave me life by causing my mama such terrible suffering. I would still like to meet him, though. First, no one can change what happened during those months of killing. Second, my Christian faith tempers the bad feelings I have toward him. Would I forgive him? Does a daughter forgive the man who gave her life? Would I try to understand him? I don't know if I would ask him questions. If I saw him, I don't know . . . I think I would greet him the way a daughter greets her father. I would ask him where he lives, in which region, his job. I would want to know why he waited so long to make himself known, whether he was imprisoned like so many others of his kind. For my part, we would have to avoid talking about Claudine and about their past. Basically, I don't know. Maybe no words would come to my lips, only trembling.

The more we dwell on all that, the heavier the pain of our past becomes. I'm not looking to forget my history or leave it behind, just don't bug me about it anymore! Just forget about me! I even wish they'd stop talking about all those things on the radio and TV. During the Week of Mourning—silence. I understand the survivors who can't accept keeping quiet. Me, I can. I yearn for silence. Survivors like to share their intimate feelings with other survivors, which is understandable. They pour out their sorrows, but me, no. Do I relieve mine by divulging the secret of my birth? My history isn't like other people's. When they discuss the killings and show pictures, it's as if they were passing a blade across a deep inner wound. Still, I don't at all feel reluctant to talk to you. There's nothing risky about a *muzungu*'s book, because not everyone reads it.* The people who buy it don't blabber on saying nasty things—or do they? On the other hand, repeating something so abnormal for the neighbors' ears, that would be

---

*Etymologically, the term *muzungu* means "one who takes the place of others." It popularly refers to a white person.

harmful. All these thoughts quicken the sadness of the girl who is revealing them to you, and I get mixed up.

Deep down, I feel trapped, as I said. Sometimes I wish I could hide from the words that tell my story so I could keep the sadness away. I don't want this melancholy. I don't want to hear another word. What happened sullies me with shame. I don't want to see anything anymore in those mocking looks. But instead I sometimes see only my mama dragged by force through the depths of distress. She told me about the marshes, her misfortune in Congo. She answered my questions, even the ones that must have tortured her. So much gratitude and goodness bring tears to my eyes. I want to show her, and to tell everyone. That's why I don't know which to choose: to speak or to keep silent about my situation.

IN RILIMA

ON THE ROAD TO BURUNDI, A PATH BREAKS OFF into the dust of the arid Bugesera toward Rilima. At the Gako military base, one leaves the last of the eucalyptus forests behind. The savanna grasses begin to grow yellow and short, the scraggly bushes knot, and first the banana groves and then the bean fields disappear. An undulating ocher expanse opens out under the dazzling sun for as far as the eye can see. At a certain point, the path plunges down toward the shore of a lake. Crocodiles slide through a tangle of aquatic grasses without rippling the water on the lookout for incautious birds and, as rumor has it, unfortunate fishermen.

People say that forty years ago the pastures belonged to free-ranging buffalo herds. Visitors crossed paths with elephants, pythons, and the occasional lion. Today, sinewy Ankole cattle graze in the bush, nodding their long, lyre-shaped horns, which attest to their noble bloodlines and account for their resistance to thirst.* Thanks to their valiant pedigree, they have been exempted

---

*Ankole is a cattle breed of medium size, thin and sinewy, known for its splendid lyre-shaped horns and small cervical hump. Its coat is often the color of mahogany or pied gray, black, and white. Tutsis long held the exclusive privilege of breeding Ankoles,

from the country's agricultural reforms, and needn't bother with cowsheds, road crossings, or ropes tied to trees. Nothing has changed since my last trip through here. The ocher earth surrounds squares of green crops, whose water points draw women, often young girls, walking single file to fill the jerry cans they carry on their heads or on their bicycles.

The penitentiary's high beige walls overlook the landscape from atop a hill. A gate has replaced the former barrier of a simple rope, and flower-bedecked parking lots now welcome the SUVs of VIP visitors from the Red Cross, the UN, and various other humanitarian organizations. A crowd of women and children have settled under a cluster of trees beside the prison walls. They chat in small groups amid heaps of bundles from home. Some have lit fires and set out their cooking pots; a good many are asleep on mats. The women here rose before sunrise to arrive in time for visiting hours, carrying supplies or documents for their men to sign.

Nearby, pink-uniformed inmates attend to water duties, weed the flower beds, and unload the trucks. Farther off, on the esplanade from which a path leads down to the lake, a group of squatting prisoners, tools over their shoulders, await the whistle signaling them to depart for the prison plantations, which extend over several dozen acres. The men will return in the evening intoning work songs, their shoulders bent under sacks filled to feed their fellow inmates and enrich the prison administration.

On a blackboard in the intendent's office, the figures for the day's population are written out in chalk: 2,574 *génocidaires*, including 101 women, and 497 common criminals, 71 of whom are

---

which they used more as symbols of wealth and as offerings than for consumption. Almost entirely wiped out during the genocide, the breed now exceeds its pre-1994 numbers. Land reforms designed to modernize rearing practices have aimed to cross-breed Ankole herds, to distribute them more evenly, and, above all, to allocate the cattle to individual families in line with the government's slogan "one family, one cow."

over seventy years old. Although the prison population has decreased by two-thirds since the presidential pardons in 2003, the clamor one hears from within the walls hasn't diminished. The din of beating drums can't quite drown out the rhythms of booming hymns; the muezzins' calls still vie with the preachers' sermons; the church choirs compete with the shouts from volleyball games and the syncopated singing of inmates at work.

Only two men remain from the group of prisoners who spoke in *Machete Season*: Fulgence Bunani, who was sent back to prison following a *gaçaça* trial, and Joseph-Désiré Bitero, whose death sentence was commuted to a life term. His daughter Fabiola had earlier jumped into my van to join me. The wait drags on. She grows restless, not knowing if her father will be allowed to come out, and anxious, too, about making the most of the few minutes authorized for their visit. She was four years old when her father was imprisoned. She attends a technical high school near Kibungo Prefecture. She is a beautiful young girl, at once cheerful and timid. In an ordinary family, she would have been strolling arm in arm with a sweetheart and perhaps by now a husband. Instead, she is by herself and stays constantly on her guard. One can sense her suspicions, but her distrust no doubt has less to do with people per se than with the way they look at her.

She expressed no hesitation about telling her story. On the contrary, she seized the occasion of our interviews to share her experiences, which she had long kept buried in herself. She didn't finagle her way out of answering and she didn't impose conditions on my questions, as I had feared. She shares her mother's plaintive voice, which has become a way for her to convey her uneasiness. One rarely sees her in Nyamata, except at the market or occasionally at the Cultural Center; she won't be found with a group of girlfriends. She takes on odd jobs during school vacations, sometimes on building sites. Otherwise she spends her time at home. Her gaze, like that of her brother Fabrice, hints at past hardships.

Joseph-Désiré finally arrives, approaching with the rolling gait of someone accustomed to being watched. He has a stout and supple sway to the shoulders and wears white sneakers a touch less chic than the boxing shoes he sported during our last visit. Although his star as an *interahamwe* chief has waned among the prisoners, his popularity surprisingly persists. He remains for everyone the same man he has always been. He lingers in long hearty greetings. His eighteen years of prison have scarcely left a trace. The region's fresh dry air and the prohibition on alcohol undoubtedly compensate for the effects of living in such close quarters. He has hardly gained a pound; he sleeps well, has good digestion, and suffers only from rheumatism and from fevers during malaria epidemics. "Things seem to be going all right," he says. "I've gotten used to this life, spending my days keeping my mind busy on pointless things." All the same, a certain weariness emerges from his words; the firmness of conviction that was once so recognizable in him seems to have flagged. For years he expended his energy on refining his rhetoric, filing appeals, contesting evidential points, and decrying procedural errors. Although the strict logic of his thought would doubtless rule out the possibility, he probably senses that his litigiousness eventually undermined any hope of benefiting from the government's policy of reconciliation. He may suspect—although he has always been a difficult man to read—that by rejecting contrition, by ignoring his victims, by refusing to open his eyes to the past, indeed, by endlessly calculating, he badly miscalculated.

A number of years ago, in the little garden near the prison wall, he explained to me: "Any civilized person must take responsibility for his actions. However, life sometimes presents us with actions that one can't admit to out loud. Me, I was the leader of the *interahamwe* for the district . . . I assumed that responsibility. Not everyone is capable of acknowledging such a truth. Confessing to such a serious sin demands more than courage. And telling the details of something so extraordinary can be sheer hell—for the person who does the telling as well as for those who listen. Because afterward, if you have revealed a situation that society refuses to believe, a truth that society considers inconceivable, it may hate you beyond all measure . . . A man is a man, even on death row. If he has the opportunity to keep quiet about a terrible, or even diabolical, truth, he will try to keep that truth quiet forever. Too bad if his silence relegates him to the status of a savage brute."

If there is a time when one knows he is being sincere, it is when he expresses his regrets as a father and teacher for having ruined his children's education. As he told me one day, explaining why he returned from Congo after two years of exile, aware that a death sentence inevitably awaited him in Nyamata: "I knew that the prisons were overflowing and that a good many people were dying there. But I wanted to return to my country so that my family might still have the chance at an ordinary life on the parcel. I didn't want my daughters to end up like some shabby derelicts in a faraway forest."

FABIOLA MUKAYISHIMIRE

NINETEEN YEARS OLD

Daughter of Joseph-Désiré Bitero, Hutu prisoner

YOU KNOW GATARE, THE TEACHERS' NEIGHBORHOOD in Nyamata. That's where I was born. We lived there in the first house built in brick because my papa aspired to be a prominent person. In reality, I grew up near Kanazi, in a cob-walled place, the one with the rusted sheet metal you see along the road, where our family settled after we returned from Congo. Not a single memory has stuck with me from our escape to the Congolese camp. I was a little girl. I can recite like a schoolgirl the twists and turns of the panicked journey they talk about, the camps that opened their arms to us at the foot of the volcano. I have forgotten personal details, except that we ate a lot of cookies and that we were surrounded by black lava everywhere we looked. I think we children went to the outdoor preschool, we played with traditional balls made of banana leaves. We lived in plastic-sheet tents—I've seen them in photos.

I remember many aggravations from after we returned to Nyamata because I endured them throughout my childhood. Papa had gone off to prison, and Mama raised the hoe from morning to night. We were forbidden from entering the neighbors' yards. We had to entertain ourselves within our enclosure, without dillydallying along the way. We made do by ourselves. I jumped rope, I played soccer with my brothers. Since then, my fondness for soccer has always stayed with me. I am skillful at playing; I watch the matches when I can. What holidays or ceremonies do I remember? Dancing at an uncle's wedding was memorable. Yes, there's that, because it was our first visit. I also won't forget the Sunday of my confirmation, when I wore a white dress like so many other girls.

We were thrilled by the mass at Christmas every year. We put aside our worn-out clothes. We went to church in fine order, then continued the vigil at home. My mama served quite extraordinary meals, like rice with grilled sweet potatoes and gravy. No one invited us, not even our aunt from Nyamata, who was a well-to-do nurse. The days of the Nativity, we weren't allowed to have fun with the families next door. Joy made itself scarce. Danger loomed everywhere. Neighbors hurled all kinds of threats and grumbled about revenge. We were too little to measure the actual malice of the neighborhood folks. We avoided them.

Our whole ethnicity has gotten a terrible reputation, but in our family, we know we are seen as worse than the others. We pay for sins we didn't commit. And there is no way to fight back because it has to do with Papa. It's uncomfortable to admit and unthinkable to complain. Anyway, complain to whom? We keep it inside, the sadness in the soul.

Years ago, my mama was a nurse's aide at the Nyamata maternity clinic. Since Congo, though, she farms to survive. She works the hoe but makes no profit from the land. It's obvious that farming disgusts her. When she despairs, she gives up the hoe. She has headaches. When a child annoys her or when a neighbor offends her, or when a drought lasts, her troubles become so overwhelming we have to take her to the hospital for psychiatric care. I feel endlessly sorry for Mama. Myself, I don't suffer from anxiety, but her difficulties pain me all the same.

We children are the only ones who stand by her. No relatives come to her aid, as tradition says they should, not even with little gifts or small sums of money. We no longer see our relatives. Some didn't come back from Congo, others chose to stay in Gitarama without ever returning to Nyamata, and, of course, most are just as needy as we are. They steer clear of our parcel. People in our family don't love each other like before. In Africa, if you find yourself without a family, it's a big thing. The same goes for acquaintances. They no longer sneak away a few minutes to stop in, especially if the rains are short or some misfortune is hanging over their homes. My papa's former colleagues don't dare drop by to say hello. His death sentence frightens them. Basically, people fear nasty looks if they come to our door. They finagled their penance, they humble themselves before the gaze of the authorities, and they fear being suspected of negationism. We manage on our own. Once you have been abandoned by everyone, you get used to not expecting the mutual support that tradition demands.

MY NAME IS Fabiola Mukayishimire. It means "thanks be to God." I am nineteen years old. When I was a little girl, the rumors vexed me without my ever imagining what really happened. When I was more grown up, I insisted on knowing why Papa was never coming back. Mama lied: He had left for a faraway voyage. He works nonstop for a successful company. He is going to bring the whole family to the new place where he lives. Fabrice and I continued to worry. Since we repeated the questions about Papa's extraordinary absence, she finally admitted that he was in prison. I was seven years old. We asked why he had been imprisoned, and she replied that they kept him there like nearly all the papas from the hills. Why? She weaved her way through explanations.

It was at primary school that I began to understand. During history lessons, classmates from the other ethnicity questioned the teachers about what had happened. The teachers explained the killings. Did my classmates turn around to look at me? I don't remember anything surprising. Wickedness never touched me at school in Kanazi. The pupils didn't know very much about my papa because we had been in Nyamata during the events. I'm not sure if this is also how it was for my older brother Fabrice. Anyway, I myself was never pestered with nasty words. I learned about the ethnic conflict in class. I found out some information about the killings, and later about the escape to Congo, the trials of the ones who confessed. The teachers delivered their lesson without adding personal details about the culprits or the dead. No mention of names or relatives. We didn't talk about it at home. We turned the dial on the radio to avoid the commemorative programs. That was a rough time for us. I was brought to the memorial site with my school. I heard witness accounts during the ceremonies. Which ones? The stories about the people burned in the church. The people thrown into pits, the looted houses, the expeditions in places like the Nyamwiza marshes.

My brother and I connected all that with Papa's punishment. One morning, point-blank, I asked my mama if Papa had done something terrible. She told me that he hadn't killed anyone. I persisted with the stubbornness of a little girl. She explained that he had kept his machete from the blood, but that he had been a famous guide. We lived that way for a long time, without really knowing if Papa wielded his machete or not. The rumors flew; with Papa gone, they kept us from digging too deep. When a child ponders things with no adult to support her, she feels uneasy and she loses trust. In other words, she stops listening. In 2003, we heard that the other children's papas were leaving prison in a long line of pardoned men. We wondered why Papa wasn't one of them. But really, we wondered why, if Papa hadn't killed with his blade, he had been given the death penalty.

That's just the life we children lived: in dread of knowing what happened and what was going to happen to our papa. Fabrice, too, started questioning again. When nothing was going right at home—for example when sickness came, when drought ate away the land—we exchanged restless or comforting words. We shared our thoughts: Why isn't Papa here? Is he ever coming back? And if Papa was here, how our lives would improve. That's how we spoke to each other in difficult times.

MY PAPA'S NAME is Joseph-Désiré Bitero. He used to teach at the Nyamata school. They said he was jovial and very mild-mannered. Everyone knows his name in Nyamata because he led the young *interahamwe* in Habyarimana's party. I was too young to attend his trial in 1996, when he received the death sentence. I know that afterward people testified against him during the *gaçaças*, but I didn't go to listen. The first time I visited him in Rilima? I was in my fifth year of primary school, eleven years old.

It was good to see my papa. He seemed kind, very strong, affectionate. He showed he was a good papa. Did I ask him any questions? Does a little girl dare ask a personal question of her prisoner father? Even now, at nineteen years old, I keep from asking him about his past doings. I go to Rilima when I can, on weekends, otherwise during school vacations. Sometimes I take a bike-taxi, and sometimes my brothers rent a bicycle and bring me along. The route takes several hours; we hold out hope for a five-minute chat. If the crowd jostling to get in is too big, the guards cut two minutes off the visits.

Papa asks how things are going at school. We exchange quick bits of news. I ask him if his health is as he would like it to be.

At the prison, things are a mess. Visitors poke their ears into our conversations; we don't have the chance to talk privately with Papa. He always has a smile for me. He never mentions the genocide. He used to speak a little about the *gaçaças*, about the steps he was taking, about the letters he was writing to the high court in order to have the decision overturned. He hinted at changes in people's attitudes. We don't speak about it anymore. No, he has never picked up his pen to write me the truth: "Listen, Fabiola, you are grown up enough to understand, this is why I have been punished . . ." No. I think it's too beneath him. He and his conscience fight over his past. He writes to encourage us to grow up brave. He believes that God is going to lend a hand in his release. In Rilima, he devotes himself to God, he implores us to give Him thanks, and he sings hallelujahs at the top of his lungs, which rise up into the sky. He shows his repentance. He tries to raise our spirits. He insists that we study without distractions at school.

I AM A boarder in my second-to-last year at the secondary school in Gitarama. It's a scientific institution, where I study mathematics, economics, and geography. I get up and shower at four-thirty, study at five o'clock. At six we gather to clean the grounds, and lessons start at seven, last until two o'clock, then lunchtime. In the afternoon, we amuse ourselves with various activities like sports and television. At seven o'clock, study, followed by the evening meal. On weekends, we are given more time for recreation—soccer, which I play without fail, and music. We rehearse songs in chorus, we watch movies. Myself, I'm fond of videos of love songs. I really enjoy romantic shows, like Indian series. The actors I admire the most are Indian, because they play romantic roles. They show affection and a good education, and they never shout impolite things at each other. They love with passion and they dress with style. I stay away from war stories, like violent American films.

The school makes computers available, which allow us to learn about computer science and the internet. I've created a Facebook profile, which doesn't have a lot of friends yet. I'm not as active as the other girls, only on the sly. Anyway, at school we are forbidden to waste our time on it, and I don't have the pocket money to break the rules at an internet café. I have a lot of school friends. Like normal girls, we talk about everything, about ourselves, our futures, our fashion obsessions, our secret whims and private thoughts, and boys, of course, because it's a coed school. The boys show off and strut around; we make fun of them without their noticing. We never bring up our parents.

No one talks about the genocide at school. We're boarders—we don't know one another's families, and there is no mention of ethnicities. Thanks to the long road separating us from Nyamata, no one has heard of Joseph-Désiré Bitero. We don't quarrel. I know that careless words might offend one friend of mine, so I prefer not to risk troubling her with secrets. Not a single Tutsi student has ever come up to me to talk about the genocide, even by accident.

In Kanazi, I stayed silent around schoolmates. When I'm in groups, I try not to stand out, I throw myself into fun activities so as to forget the past. Sometimes I think about my mama, who lives alone farming to feed the family. The constant search for money bends a mama's back. It upsets me more at school than it does at home. My mind drifts off into nostalgic thoughts. Worries lose me points on my exams. In my school, survivor children receive aid from the FARG, the Genocide Survivors Support and Assistance Fund.* It

---

*Since its creation in 1998, the Genocide Survivors Support and Assistance Fund (Fonds d'aide aux rescapés du génocide), which represents approximately 5 percent of Rwanda's annual budget, has, among other things, financed the education of around fifty thousand high school students and seven thousand university student survivors.

pays the *minervals* when the need arises. Life is meant to be easier for those students than it is for me, despite the deaths they have suffered through. Everyone can see that they grow up more comfortably. They feel innocent, they aren't ashamed of their loved ones. They know that others view them more positively than me. I'm nostalgic for an optimistic life.

So I pray like everyone else. I had a Catholic baptism. I beg the dear Lord to improve my family's hard existence. At church, I avoid choir and charitable activities but not God. I have been devout ever since I was very little. I have never dreamt of giving it up, I have never faltered. I pray for Rwandan unity and for my papa to be released very soon. God knew what was happening on the hills, but He provided human beings with the intelligence to choose between Good and Evil. He gave them the ability to recognize sin and to determine their own actions. The priests at church use veiled words to evoke the extermination. They speak about it in terms of morality. They console their flock, people who have lost so much or who have been mired in misfortune. They also preach against the genocidal ideology of the former government's decrees. At school, young people avoid sharing their thoughts about God. If someone brings up the problem of Evil in one of our conversations, we are careful not to blame Him. We fear God.

SIDESADDLE ON A BIKE-TAXI

THE OLD KIGALI ROAD, WHICH WAS ONCE SO PITTED and broken it had to be driven in first gear, today runs smooth and paved all the way to Burundi. Storm gutters line its sides as it passes through Nyamata. At dusk, streetlights sometimes draw enough electricity to illuminate it. During the night, sentries' mute silhouettes mind the route's main intersections.

Within a new, bright-red service station, Mimi has opened a swank cabaret-boutique. She is one of the innumerable adoptive children of Marie-Louise, who found the stray Mimi along the Gitarama road in the upheaval following the genocide. Mimi has inherited her adoptive mother's entrepreneurial spirit and lucky hand in business. She sometimes returns exhausted from her boutique to join Marie-Louise's crowded table for dinner.

Although two banks built side by side now block Marie-Louise's view of the comings and goings of the street, the seclusion hasn't affected her intrinsic understanding of Nyamata. For Marie-Louise Kagoyire knows everything. From morning till night, acquaintances drop in to see her. Friends of the youngsters living with her set themselves down on her long table's benches. A parade of people pass by to say hello on market days.

If a story has been making the rounds at the cabaret Heaven, a visitor comes to recount it to her. If the district reaches an official decision, a guest reports the details. If the banana trees are withering in Mayange, she knows all about it even before you have come back to bring her the news. People are well aware of her generosity and gourmets know all about her talents in the kitchen. Men and women come from far up on the hills to avail themselves of her wisdom and on occasion her influence. She is present at all the funerals, and she is required at all the baptisms. Every Saturday she leaves for a wedding, which often takes her as far as Kigali. Always discreet, she refuses to divulge how many people she has married off. She remains a past master of the long-winded negotiations, smooth talking, and hazards that precede the wedding vows. When in doubt she goes in person or picks up her mobile phone. And then there is the retinue of her adoptive children.

She began taking them in just after the killings. There was Mimi, who had made her way to Gitarama on foot; Yvette and Adam, running down the town's main street; Jean-Baptiste, holed up in an orphanage; then her own family's children or those of her deceased husband's family—Irène, Diane, Jean-Paul, and many others. Her home has long echoed with the sounds of her vast brood of children, about whom she says: "We have helped each other a lot. It isn't easy raising orphans. I can say, though, that they have helped me more than I have helped them by being their mama. Being alone after the genocide would have been unbearable to me. I don't know if they see themselves as brothers and sisters. But I think it would be impossible for one of the boys to fall in love with one of the girls, or vice versa, because they live with each other as brothers and sisters. And what if it did happen? It hasn't happened yet."

She has already married many of them off: Denise, Jean-Paul,

Diane, Yvette, Fils, and soon Emmanuel and Médiatrice. The ones who have left speak French, while those who have taken over their bedrooms speak English: Adam goes to a school set up by Israelis, tall Prudence expects to be tapped by the national volleyball team, little Pascaline courageously struggles against a nasty illness, Médiatrice works in a newsroom, Emmanuel is looking for a job. Although the two banks' generators have chased away the birds that once clamored in the courtyard, they haven't diminished the racket one hears at daybreak as the whole family washes up.

IN ADDITION TO her cabaret-boutique, Mimi manages a cooperative farther down the street, across from the hardware store Vision Idéale, the cabaret Blue Star, the restaurant Le Petit Bazar, and the Beauty Saloon. The shop signs are part of the linguistic battle that continues to rage. While the hardware stores, groceries, and pharmacies have tended to remain francophone, the banks, large cabarets, hair salons, cell phone shops—everything else, in fact—have been switching to English. At the main intersection's taxi stand, motorcycles are replacing bicycles, the latter limited to long-distance trips to the hills, where the steep paths risk overheating the single-cylinder Indian motors. In Nyamata, the buses are imported from Korea, the cars from Japan; the motorbikes are made in India, the bicycles in China.

Flocks of gray geese pass in waves, their necks outstretched in aerodynamic pursuit. Cackling fills the sky. They come from Scandinavia or Russia on their way south. As for Englebert, he leaves Tite's wife's dive bar with the obvious intention of returning as soon as he can. In the meantime, he has spotted the van parked across the street. He circles it, surveys the surroundings, bemused. He smells a bottle within reach. He sets off but isn't exactly sure where to. Unable to make up his mind, he doubles back, takes another turn around the truck, scratches his head in distress, then scrutinizes the vicinity more carefully until, with relief, he finally catches sight of me at Mimi's. He scurries across the street in my direction.

A lithe, slender young girl wearing black sunglasses passes by riding sidesaddle on a bicycle's passenger seat. It's Ange, Gigi to her family, Angel on her Facebook profile. The daughter of a French professor, Innocent Rwililiza, and a francophone, Épiphanie Kayitesi, Ange speaks a lovely English, with just a touch of an East Coast accent, which isn't surprising since she attends a Catholic school managed by a foundation from Boston. She hops off the bike-taxi in front of the internet café.

ANGE UWASE

NINETEEN YEARS OLD

Daughter of Innocent Rwililiza, Tutsi survivor

THE SEMESTER ENDED WELL, SAFE FROM BAD GRADES.
I am excited about my vacation in Nyamata. Our family lives in the
Kayumba neighborhood, on the other side of the high school.
The breeze blows its cool air on the dust up there. It's good. During vacations, I like giving my mama a hand with the cleaning
work and preparing the meals. I continue playing basketball, the
same as at school. I am often asked to play center, thanks to my long
and slender build. I am not much of a dancer. I don't feel so confident when I dance. At school, dance music is banned in our rooms,
and in Nyamata, you don't see attractive cabarets where you can
dance without spending a tidy sum. I'm no worse off.

I visit my girlfriends. We meet up in the courtyard, at my place
or theirs, and sometimes share a juice. They are all good friends
from school, because that is where I spend most of my time. I
wouldn't say I have a best friend—I mean, a deeply trusted confidante. But we still talk without holding back. We watch movies
on our smartphones. We all dislike American films. We can't get
enough of Nigerian soaps, with their love stories and especially the
endless family squabbles. For my part, I don't admire any celeb-

rity in particular; I couldn't give you a name that excites me, besides singers and soccer players, of course.

I have friends who are boys, like so many other girls. We see each other but our get-togethers aren't so carefree, because of our parents, who pile on their endless warnings. We chat beside the houses, we stroll along the paths, we go off to quiet spots. Our walks sometimes take us to Nyamata's main street to check out the stores and review the new fashions. I know most of the boys from primary school, the others are good neighbors. We tease each other, we joke around, and we like to talk about what is happening in our lives. I also go on walks with my brothers and sister. There are four of us children in all. We always get along. Their company cheers me up. We go to the market, to church—we even go down to the center of Nyamata if we catch news of something fun like a soccer match or a show at the Cultural Center. If we come across a little money, we order something to drink.

Nyamata is a quiet little town. Boredom doesn't last for long. Unlike before, there are plenty of entertaining things to do—it's nice. Sometimes we go to the internet café. I have opened a Facebook account, and I post photos to my timeline. My friends and I take pictures of one another striking elegant poses, which is quite the comedy. I like looking at everyone's pictures. I chat online with classmates or former teachers. For example, an American woman from Boston has been writing to me, describing how life is good where she lives, too. We discuss videos we have seen, we share how surprised we are by all the turmoil in the world, and we express our convictions. People from my mother's family scattered around Canada send me news about the Arctic cold they have over there. I listen to good music on YouTube and the like. I don't go digging around in celebrities' private lives as much as some other girls. But I do a little bit. Their love interests, their fashions, their quarrels—it's tempting to find out those frivolous things. You-Tube lets us listen to songs we don't hear on the radio. We soak up all sorts of startling news about the world. We can see that it's sensational, but that's what attracts us. I don't waste too much time on it, though. And anyway, I avoid fatal disasters, and I steer clear of terrorist attacks—they don't interest me at all. Young people in America poke around on the internet for hours, but with us it isn't for so long.

The teachers give us thirty minutes at school. They encourage us to do research on Google to document our work. I am in my third year at Maranyundo Girls School. It's an American boarding school. Students come from everywhere. School makes me happy because we learn complex subjects, and because we can talk among us girls without the disruptions of the other sex. When I am on vacation, I only surf the internet when I have the money. It really adds up. I can go nearly a week without touching the keyboard.

I often browse sites about the genocide. It turns out that they aren't very informative. I don't linger very long. I am mostly interested in pictures. I am always eager for images of the genocide; my little girl's memory let them all fade away, so for me, they never grow old. I feel sorry for people who can't look at pictures to really understand the killings. Future generations won't have these shocking images to fight against forgetting. Don't the photos violate the victims' privacy? I can't say they don't. Too bad if sensitive people feel offended that someone might see them in a shameful situation. Me, too—I might be seen full of fright in my hiding place, or see my first papa cut and thrown alive into a common grave. Don't the photographs do an injustice to the women who hiked up their *pagnes* to their waists to run faster? The humiliation obviously adds to the pain of the memory. But I'm certain that photos refute more strongly than ceremonies the negationist words of people who aren't the least bit disgusted by the killings. That's my opinion.

MY NAME IS Ange Uwase. I don't exactly know what it means; it's pretty complicated. Born in Kigali, nineteen years ago, one year before the genocide. Afterward, I grew up in Nyamata, first in a small adobe home in Gasenga, a worthless, dingy neighborhood, if I may say so, then in this brick house in Kayumba. My first papa was killed during the genocide. My other papa's name is Innocent Rwililiza; he teaches in Nyamata. He's the one my mama chose to start a second family with. Her name is Épiphanie Kayitesi. She works a bit at the preschool, a lot on our land, and at home, of course.

I think the genocide was never very far from my childhood ears. I have always lived with this commotion. From the age of five, maybe before, I knew that people had been mistreated in a terrible event, but the words flew past without landing. When family acquaintances talked about it, or when my parents brought it up, I could see they were badly shaken. It set me to trembling, I kept my distance. The words frightened me too much for me to try to picture what they meant. The words drove me away. I refused to listen even when it was in secret, the way children usually like to listen to their parents' private conversations.

In primary school, we youngsters didn't speak about the genocide very much, and only in timid words. Who had lost their papas, their mamas, or their grandparents; who had no help, who was having a breakdown. We related all our worries without pressing too hard. There weren't any quarrels yet. It was in the last year of primary school that our teacher began history lessons. We didn't dare ask him many questions. We were too nervous to contradict him. Some students were interested in delving more deeply into things, others stayed silent—they kept to the side, as if they were sulking. Trouble snuck among the school benches without the teacher noticing.

We spoke about the genocide in our family. It was in the evenings, when everyone was settled in and the questions came thick and fast. Mama and Papa kept certain parts of the story out because of our age. When I was thirteen, I had the courage to ask more probing questions. I saved them for my mama. I always craved more details about my fate because I myself escaped the machete as an infant. In fact, I suffered during the genocide without knowing it. When did I first get this idea? I haven't got a single memory from that time. But as far back as I could remember, I had always been bothered by something pretty significant that had supposedly happened to me. Mama answered my questions very well, with no hesitation. She told me how the two of us lived in a hiding place in Kigali after my first papa's death, about the Arab neighbors who hid me during the day, where we took refuge at dusk, and how the fear returned every morning. Innocent told me about being hunted in the Kayumba forest. He didn't mention every detail, only the most vivid ones for our education.

At times, we feel comfortable enough to speak about it at home. My brothers and sister get their curiosity piqued because they were born later. Our parents recount their experiences without beating about the bush. They say they want to transmit the true story of the Tutsis to our generation. Immaculée sometimes asks me personal questions even though she knows that I was a little baby at the time. If I know, I answer honestly. Things are calm in our living room. We exchange questions and explanations. Papa doesn't care if he divulges survivors' shameful secrets: he speaks in direct words of their filthy nakedness, of the children abandoned during their parents' flight, of the ladies raped in front of people's eyes. Our conversations aren't rushed. I can talk about it with

Mama for an entire day. I am curious about all the stories and to learn the details of people's existence during the killings and how they escaped. I want to know the most unforgettable moments, how people constantly helped each other, their nighttime prayers together, the silence in their hiding places. I am always looking to pick up new information. The story of the marshes, the hunts in the forests, the hideout in Kigali. There's no end to my questions.

Have I gone up to the Kayumba forest where my papa fled? No, and I haven't visited the house of our Arab neighbors in Kigali, either. I keep from visiting those places, as well as the memorials. I keep away from public ceremonies. I avoid the hubbub of the crowds. I am afraid of the fainting spells, the people weeping, the dramatic gestures.

My brothers and sister and I talk openly. That hardly ever happens among young people. Sometimes it happens with friends by accident. What I mean is, if a person is suddenly in the grip of a crisis, we go off to the side to share our experiences and express our feelings. It's a way of bringing out before the others' eyes a bit of what each of us has been through. But we avoid going too deeply into private matters. With the children of the other ethnicity—I am thinking of girlfriends from school—we pass over all that, except during memorial visits. In that case, on the walk there, you choose careful words so as not to upset the other person.

I have Hutu girlfriends at school. Not one has ever come up to me to ask a simple question about how my family escaped the killings or about the existence I myself have had to endure. Why not? I think I know. Young Hutus know the details of the genocide. They learned them at school, they have listened to some of the radio programs. They have heard the melancholy songs. But they shy away from the questions they ought to ask their parents. The facts come out in fits and starts at home. They are afraid of learning what their parents' involvement was, or they know the reason their papa was put in prison, but they have never heard their families confirm it. There are some who pretend to be ignorant but really know everything.

I know some young Hutus who reject the hate that slips into their families' explanations. They put their trust in the teachers. Even so, they show less enthusiasm for information than the children of survivors. Their parents curb their curiosity. When they are together in the evenings, are those parents capable of describing how they plied the machete, or of divulging the darkest secrets of a neighbor's death in the marshes? If so, is a Hutu child then capable of treating his father as someone wicked? No one has ever heard of such a thing.

Resentment unites the two camps of young Hutus and Tutsis, not a hunger for the truth. Young Hutus hate their schoolmates, whom they suspect of favoritism. A few of them are bold enough to say in front of everyone: "I'm going to be pulled out of school because there aren't enough hands to work our land, while you get special privileges. The FARG pays the *minervals* at American schools so you can graduate without getting dirt on your hands." Their Tutsi classmates answer back: "You, you live surrounded by your family's strong arms, while orphans raise the hoe because the machetes cut their papas in the papyrus. They plow the earth for their brothers' and sisters' food. And on Sundays after church they have no one to visit because their family perished beneath the blades." School life quells their anger but not their suspicions. Distrust lurks behind their friendly greetings; it never gives way. If poverty drives Hutus or Tutsis from school, they long for revenge. It's understandable.

I don't see the future as risky or chaotic, though. The farmers' machetes no longer frighten anyone because people have gladly benefited from the policy of national reconciliation. Even still, while Hutus tend to appear kind, and to present an encouraging face, Tutsis continue to lecture their children to stay on their guard. I don't know how many generations we will go through before young Tutsis and Hutus can laugh together in sincere friendship. I mean, without fearing a sudden awkwardness. Essentially, the future depends on God's will.

NEITHER MAMA'S COURAGE nor her luck saved me; it was God's mercy. It's written in the Holy Scriptures that He created mankind. He has counted out the days of each of our lives. Mama survived because it wasn't her time to go to heaven; my first papa was cut because he was called to go. Neither of them had done more good or more bad. I'm a faithful believer. In Nyamata, I pray at the Presbyterian church. At school, I go to the Catholic church because it is a Catholic school. I find God just as easily among Protestants as among Catholics. The genocide has no influence on my faith. Innocent people were killed, children suffered, poor people were cut, and yet it wasn't due to God's negligence. Nothing like that happens by accident or as punishment, or for want of love. Certain people had to die. God knew it because He knows everything.

Why didn't He reach out a helping hand, why didn't He strike the killers with lighting to stop them? It's a question that everyone asks themselves. I often wonder. The question is part of God's mystery. I survived thanks to God, while other innocent children were cut. It reinforces my faith in Him. I have heard that in terrible moments survivors renounced their faith. I can understand how they turned their backs on God. Questioning His existence is common sense when you are in the forest fleeing the machete from morning to night. Those believers really were trapped, pleading, their hands reaching out for help or a merciful sign that never came. There were some who begged to die as Christians, to kneel on dry land and say a short prayer, without being allowed even that much. Others chose to take refuge in churches, where slaughter awaited them, and still others were traumatized by the behavior of ringleader priests. Their anger is legitimate, and I could never condemn it.

In my heart of hearts, it isn't something I share, because then the questions it raises end up tormenting me. Faith doesn't reassure. It doesn't soothe the anguish of having nearly been exterminated. The church isn't there to make us forget such an extraordinary event. Believing in God to find some relief—that isn't something that lasts. I honestly think that God saved me. Many survivors believe the same. Many Hutus believe that God helped them return alive from their exodus in order to begin a new life in peace. We pray. I sing in the choir at church and at school. I sing very well. Singing brings me joy. Exuberant guitars sweep us along behind synthesizers and drums. That offers hope, anyway.

HANGING AROUND ON MAIN STREET

EVERYONE IS IN A PANIC THIS MORNING AT
Marie-Chantal's. The faces are solemn, attending the lamenta-
tions of the mistress of the house as she beseeches heaven for
help. She denounces the wide range of evil spirits that have perse-
cuted her over the years. Her daughter Fabiola does her best to
calm Marie-Chantal down as inquisitive neighbors observe the
drama from behind the hedgerow. Last night the family cow disappeared, its halter left lying at the foot of a tree. Someone had to
have heard it galloping off. Certain of those present thought the cow
must have returned to the rancher who sold it to her, but one
of Marie-Chantal's sons comes back empty-handed. He sets out
again, this time with his brother, to scour the bush. Others insist
that a curse must have driven the cow mad. But why the curse?
Still others maintain that the apparent disappearance is merely
meant to cover up a death due to negligence. (The one cow that
each family receives as part of Rwanda's agricultural reforms isn't
replaced in the case of mistreatment.) The most suspicious among
them say that the animal was probably sold.

Nothing ever goes well in this house. Two days earlier it was
a problem with one of her sons, who had to be taken to the clinic

with severe stomach pains. Had he been poisoned? Not long before that, sheet metal broke off their roof during a rainstorm. No one in Nyamata complains more than Marie-Chantal. This has been going on for quite some time—since the end of the genocide.

She had married a teacher from a good family, a tall, strong, cheerful man who swiftly climbed the ranks of Habyarimana's organization to become head of the party's youth movement. She grew a taste for life among Gatare's notables. She gloated over the timorous glances people cast at the wife of the *intera-hamwe* chief, Joseph-Désiré Bitero. She was seen strutting around during the killings, in the streets and at the maternity hospital where she worked. But then disaster hit. In less time than it takes to describe, she found herself barefoot on the road to the Congolese camps. And once she returned from exile, there she was: the wife of a horrible bastard, a woman who had shamelessly exploited her position. She was obliged to move to an adobe hut and take up the hoe to feed her children.

Nowadays, no one loiters at the church as much as Marie-Chantal in her bid for the priest's pity. She faithfully frequents local charities, bemoans her misery in the clinic courtyard, and collects all the public assistance she can at the district offices. She wears her poverty on her clothes, a poverty verging on destitution. It would be an understatement to say that she remains ignorant of the discreet elegance of the poor as they go, dignity intact, to the market or a ceremony. She drags out her misfortune with the brazenness of someone incapable of sparing a thought for the women around her, including those women whose husbands were cut down in the marshes.

Her daughter Fabiola doesn't follow in her footsteps. One hardly ever sees them together in central Nyamata. Instead, with her timid gait, she tries to fade into the background, even though she feels compassion for her mother and is quick to say so. She stands by Marie-Chantal, and clearly feels deeply grateful to her for having raised her through adversity.

The attitude of her son, Fabrice, makes it difficult to gauge his feelings. He doesn't complain, never rebels, and asks for nothing. He makes himself scarce. Expelled from school, because, he says, tuition was too expensive for them at the time, he now refuses to join in farming the family land. At most he might lend a hand weeding or at harvesttime. He leaves the house early in the morning and returns only to eat at night. He is trying to make a go of it in Kigali, where he sometimes spends several weeks whenever he scrapes together enough to pay for the ticket. Otherwise, he wanders Nyamata. He doesn't have the money for a Primus in the big cabarets like Heaven, Heroes, or Red Lion, where young people his age meet. He doesn't care enough for *urwagwa* to be enticed by the dive bars. He hangs around on the main street dressed in his American shirt, jeans, and tennis shoes. He shoots the breeze, takes on odd jobs here and there, and shows real grit, especially in restaurant work, where hiring comes just as fast as firing because the owners, often Tutsis, presumably don't cut him many breaks. He sometimes goes to Nyamata's concert venue or, more accurately, its dimly lit den, where, in sauna like humidity, sports fans gather to watch the English Premier League. Fabrice loves soccer, although soccer hasn't exactly reciprocated. On Sundays, he meets colleagues at the field when Bugesera FC has a match. With his powerful legs, exceptional quickness on the wing, nimble dribbling, and deft left foot, he probably would have had enough talent to be a standout for the Bugesera club, earning bonuses and savoring the applause, had he been able to participate in practice. He makes do playing intervillage matches in the Kanazi meadows.

He was five years old at the time of the killings, an age when childhood memories become engraved. Although he spent all his time closed up with his family in the yard of their house in Gatare, it is unfortunate that he keeps his memories to himself. He prefers to talk about the escape to Congo. What he remembers of it is quite surprising. He visits his father every month, but they never have more than five minutes to talk. It is difficult to know what he thinks of his father's role as head of the *interahamwe*, or how he feels, for example, when someone mentions his actions in leading the attack at the church. How does he make sense of his father's negationist self-defense at Rilima? Not once during our conversations does he reveal a hint of complicity with or reproach for his father. He is trying to draw out a thread among his childhood memories, something to hang on to from a time when his life was, to say the least, turned upside down. Like all other young Hutus, he has trouble understanding why others might be interested.

FABRICE TUYISHIMIRE

TWENTY-TWO YEARS OLD

Son of Joseph-Désiré Bitero, Hutu prisoner

WHAT I ESPECIALLY REMEMBER FROM THE TIME of the genocide is that we no longer went to school. In the beginning, my parents brought us to the nursery. Then the guns began to crackle and we stopped. I stayed in the yard all day. I was happy enough. There was my mama, my grandmama, and my sister Fabiola, who was just a little girl. The truck would pull up with colleagues and honk, and Papa cracked jokes with us before he climbed in. He seemed cheerful as usual.

We lived in Gatare, in the teachers' neighborhood. It was the first brick building. Tall trees shaded the yard. I don't know anymore what we grew, but flowery hedges and banana trees, anyway. The war raged elsewhere. We didn't know much about it because we were little, except for hearing the racket of honking and shouting. Nothing frightened us, no danger lurked. We enjoyed our time as a family. Do I remember what the adults said about the situation? No, we children played outside. It really was peaceful.

One lasting memory is the frantic escape later on. We bolted from home. I obviously remember that. It was nothing but shouts and screams, each one louder than the next. The mamas stuffed their bundles full, the men took down the houses' sheet metal. We rushed off, loaded with the kitchen utensils and all the supplies our backs could carry. The animals we managed to round up we pressed into a few scanty herds. We took our place in the crush of people and walked all day long. Escapees followed the line of vehicles, others disappeared in the bush. At night, we stopped in small groups and broke firewood to eat warm food. We slept in abandoned streets or in fields—it was up to the fatigue.

We were back on our feet in the morning. The mamas carried the provisions on their heads and attached the babies to their backs. Me, I was sat on my papa's shoulders or pulled by the arm. We advanced with the crush of people down the road. There were screams—we raced to escape the sound of gunshots. Those sick with malaria were carried atop bound branches because time was too short to care for them. Those sick with cholera stayed in the shade to die.

One day we crossed a river along the border. That's where Congo awaited us. We shared the pastures with the animal herds, then we were moved onto black-lava slopes where people had almost nothing to farm. White UN trucks brought sacks of food. Children gathered on a field to battle one another in traditional games. We got used to spending our days kicking the ball around. I was very skilled at dribbling with both feet. Since Papa had been a teacher, he sometimes sat us down on a school bench to give us lessons.

I knew the camp wasn't our native country. I hadn't forgotten the hills—I missed them terribly. If a child finds a place to eat and sleep in peace, and to play with friends, his carefree life outruns his memories. Then one day the war encircled our camp. There was a terrible roar of cannons and guns. The panic was unrelenting. We saw the army of uniforms. People were running in every direction but had nowhere to escape. They banged into one another to the sounds of bombshells. We came upon dead people who had hardly been mourned, and we watched moaning bloody bodies being carted away.

An unforgettable crowd urged us along like cattle. We clambered into the backs of hauling trucks. We traveled. We saw our country, Rwanda. The vehicle dropped us inside the Nyamata district, where the authorities warned us to return home. We didn't go back to our house in Gatare. I think some people had taken it for themselves. Papa decided to bring us to Kanazi, where an aunt lent us the adobe house we live in today. The World Food Programme distributed provisions. We survived, going days without leaving the enclosure. We got by with the food from our family plot.

One day a neighbor came to visit. Papa walked him out to the footpath, as is the custom. A car pulled up in front of them, and men rushed out, tied my papa's hands, and took him to the district jail. He was imprisoned in Rilima. That's how he left us, in '96. We weren't very surprised, because every day soldiers rounded up a great many people suspected of genocide.

Myself, I couldn't say if he participated in the expeditions. I remember him at home during the killings. He behaved calmly with my mama and my grandmama. I haven't forgotten how he vanished in the van. Did I see a machete at home? Not a single memory. These were things without importance for the little boy that I was at the time. When they led my papa away, I didn't understand why. It didn't upset me. As I told you, we weren't the only ones to lose a papa. They locked them up from all over—we heard about it every day. They even took mamas away. The children learned to live a new existence. They had gotten used to life in the Congo camps and they continued getting used to the tough luck that came crashing down on their families. In the end, you accept everything when you're a child.

. . .

MY NAME IS Fabrice Tuyishimire. It means "let us give thanks to the good Lord." I am twenty-two years old. I haven't forgotten the date. There are three of us boys and two girls in the family. My mama's name is Marie-Chantal Munkaka. She used to help care for women at the maternity hospital; today she farms the parcel. My papa's name is Joseph-Désiré Bitero. He received the death sentence in '96 at the Nyamata court. They didn't shoot him with the six other convicts we saw fall in broad daylight in Kayumba. They didn't release him later with the line of repentant prisoners. He lives at the penitentiary. Me, I grew up in Kanazi. I went to the primary school, I completed three years of secondary, then I quit to earn money. I missed the exams. I saw that I was too far behind to begin again.

I am no longer a student, because of a lack of *minervals* as much as a lack of attention in class. When I broke the news to my father in Rilima, he went silent. His teacher's eyes turned away. He could find nothing to say. I am getting by now. Jobs await me here and there. I help out in the cabarets and restaurants: I work as a server or bartender or do odd jobs. Some bosses are nice and keep me on long-term, others throw me out whenever there aren't enough customers. I also get hired on construction sites, as an assistant bricklayer, for example. I sometimes lend a hand weeding the crops on the family parcel, but then I take it back. I don't think much of farming. In Rwanda, farming wears out your arms so much you can't join in the country's development, which is expanding everywhere.

I play soccer very skillfully. People cheer for me. I used to kick the ball around with my childhood feet as much as I could. Then I was trained by a Congolese coach named Noa. He had us practice complex techniques. I dribble, I pass, I don't miss opportunities to score to help the team. The position where I am most comfortable is left wing, jersey number eleven. Soccer is my great joy. The Rwandan team's exploits give me thrills. Playing soccer makes me happy; it offers me moments of cheerful friendship. Later on, however, the jobs ate away at my training time and I missed my chance to wear the backup squad jersey for Bugesera FC. Now I play on the Kanazi team, which competes against other *mudugudus*. I go to Nyamata to see games. It costs three hundred francs to watch the Champions League. I'm a fan of Chelsea and Barça. I like Samuel Eto'o, Didier Drogba, and, most of all, Lionel Messi. As far as movies go, I have never been. Besides Rwandan films on TV, I don't watch movies. I prefer music—R&B or Rwandan songs. On the weekends, I go dancing at the Cultural Center, which is free, except when artists from Kigali perform. I have many friends, the ones from soccer, Kanazi neighbors, acquaintances I meet in the cabarets. No one criticizes me anymore about who I am.

In Nyamata, people know my father's situation. They don't ever hassle me. No one comes looking to talk to me about my father, and I don't seek people out. No one asks me for news. Zero talk of memories—they aren't something that comes up. Even with Fabiola, we never discuss our papa's past. No troubles between brother and sister. We steer clear of it because we don't know what to say. We share news after we go to see him, and nothing more. Fabiola tells me about her life, describing the various happy events at boarding school. We try to encourage each other, and we give each other advice, but we keep from mixing in Papa's business. It's a bond between us. I couldn't tell you if we have the same opinion of him. We never quarrel, because we grew up stranded in a hostile childhood. We met mean looks. Mama heard insults from survivors' lips. We kept on our toes for years. In the end, to us children, no damage was done, only poverty. And separation, of course.

Mama brought me to Papa's trial. I listened to the people testify against him. I was too much a child to catch all the details. When we heard the death sentence, we accepted it for what it was because we couldn't do anything else. We were frightened because others sentenced to death had been hauled in front of the crowd to meet the bullets. We saw the firing squad near Kayumba. It was very loud. Unforgettable.

Deep down, fear has never left me for long. I trembled from the explosions on the road to Congo, then from the war in the camp, and later from my papa's death sentence. My biggest fear was that my mama might be imprisoned herself. Abandonment was my little boy's obsession, because the rumors never stopped. In a situation like that, where the neighbors hide their true feelings, you are afraid without knowing what of. You don't know your parents' misdeeds, but still you are subjected to the punishment for the evil done. I grew up surrounded by people driven by hidden intentions.

Suspicion flows freely among children. Another boy may seem happy by your side, then suddenly you wonder if he isn't putting on a show. With a friend who has suffered from the killings, the friendship is false. You endlessly examine people's faces. Deep down, you distrust everyone. You are wary of leaving the family circle. No relative offers Mama any help, as custom recommends. People are sorry to be related to my papa. If they ever stopped at our gate, they did so in secret, to teach us how to handle the hoe or to give us notebooks and pens, then disappeared before paying the *minerval*. That's how I learned about the genocide. Then I had lessons about it at school. I went on a class visit to the memorial. Have I gone to the marshes? No, it hasn't crossed my mind. I have seen pictures on television. No one can deny the killings anymore, or the terrible politics of the time. How would I sum it up? You want one sentence? I'd say: Habyarimana's men wanted to eliminate the Tutsis because they were afraid of losing the war; the massacres left a great many orphans; poverty has plagued families on both sides; there is no shortage of regrets.

Fortunately, time steps in to help; it improves things. I go out now without getting blamed for my family in the eyes of others. I can't pay for my papa's actions, because I was only a child. I see myself as a decent member of society. I walk upright, without shame, when I meet Papa's colleagues or people who consider him evil. I lead an honest life because it is mine, despite the bad looks. We are Hutus. Should I be ashamed of it? Can I reject my family? I walk without lowering my gaze, I crack jokes with coworkers. I like Kanazi, since that is where I grew up after we came back from Congo. I prefer Nyamata, though, which would have been my native town. It is growing rich. No matter. God chose me to be Hutu. God offers His love without exception. I pray every Sunday. Am I going to criticize the life He has given me? How am I supposed to understand His omnipotence? No, I accept His unfathomable plans, and I don't question His silence during the killings. I never miss a single mass.

THE HOUSE WITH THE CRIMSON ROOF

PAST GATARE'S LAST ROAD, EVERYTHING CHANGES. A congregation of nuns bought up the old soccer field and built shops in its place. The district offices moved into a new five-story building. The Red Lion's terrace now extends all the way to the street, facing cell phone and beauty-cream boutiques. A neon-lit service station has replaced the run-down gas pump. In Gatare, on the other hand, every bush and tree between the low adobe houses looks familiar, as do the people going about their routines within their hedge-lined courtyards, among broods of children, chickens, and goats.

The birds continue regardless, unruffled. The ashen cranes still lift their beaks to sing in the first glimmer of daybreak, followed soon after by the throaty *cooroo-cooroos* of the green turacos. As one advances in the thicket, one spots them between rays of sunlight (that is, if a mooing cow doesn't suddenly intrude), sporting their green crests and matching breasts, hopping from branch to branch as if to entice their fellows to join the choir. Then, over the rhythm of stamping pestles, as the cooking-pot smoke and the hymns of young house girls rise from the courtyards, the bush erupts in a symphony of songs, among which those of gonoleks, weavers, and bee-eaters—birds no longer heard on Gatare's main street. For along with the new asphalt and electricity, armies of pied crows have landed from Kigali, their caws overwhelming all but the swallows, which fly too high to be bothered.

A roof of crimson sheet metal sets Édiths Uwanyiligira's house apart. To my great surprise, she offers me home-distilled honey-sweet *urwagwa* left over from the young orphans' wedding she hosted the day before. Although I boarded at her place for several months, I never had the chance to taste the fruits of her talents as a distiller. Her house, a haven of cheer removed from the racket of the street, is open to all. Her hospitality flows from good-natured sanctimoniousness. In the late afternoons, a bevy of guests stop by: neighborhood women gabbing as they fill their jerry cans with water at the tap; ladies from the parish gossiping about the clergymen, who are, of course, the most frequent of Édith's visitors. She loves to hear the cooing of the priests, deacons, guitarists, and choristers, all devout parishioners who gather at her place to commune in song and prayer and sometimes laughter—because one can hardly resist Édith's mirth as their impatient eyes gaze hungrily at plates of sweets and their nostrils thrill to the kitchen's aromas.

A new priest has dropped in today for a sip of drink. It didn't take long for him to learn where he might find a fine reception. He launches into a fiery theological discussion. He is brilliant, young, and handsome, which Édith can't help noticing. Still, although she is sincerely devoted to her congregation and holds limitless admiration for the priests, she will only ever love one man on earth, her husband, who was taken from before her eyes in their frantic escape from the machetes. His name was Jean-de-Dieu Nkurunziza, about whom one pleasant evening she had this to say: "My husband and I always lived as happily as newlyweds. We had loved each other since childhood. We grew up just five hundred meters apart on the very same hill. After secondary school, we loved each other for real—we got married. The day of our wedding, I was decked out in a white embroidered dress like in the photos. A crowd of elegant and joyful people came. My husband and I loved each other more than was necessary. I was capricious. He loved me too much and even preferred that I leave the housework alone."

Sometimes, when the memory of her husband's death brings her to the brink of a bewildering void, headaches or violent fevers keep her confined to her bedroom, where she stays to avoid stumbling or collapsing in front of the children. Several days later, she will reemerge, cheerful once again.

A band of kids bustle in the courtyard, some washing up at the tap or playing stick and hoop, others plunging their hungry hands into a big plate of fufu or pestering a duck and its ducklings—just as they had during my first stay here fifteen years ago. It makes one wonder if, within the walls of this little realm, the children have aged as little as those in children's books. Except, that is, for Sandra, Édith's daughter. Fifteen years ago she was an impish little girl, looking out onto the world with big, inquisitive eyes and ruling over the horde of kids in the courtyard. She was a touch wild, always ready to bolt on her matchstick legs toward new adventures.

Today she is a slender young woman, easygoing and headstrong, as thin as her mother is plump. She inherited Édith's exuberant cheerfulness and tremendous courage, which help her to confront the neurological disorder that afflicts her.

SANDRA ISIMBI

EIGHTEEN YEARS OLD

Daughter of Édith Uwanyiligira, Tutsi survivor

I ONCE HAD THE CHANCE TO ENTER A MOVIE THEATER.
My brother, Bertrand, had come back from America, and he paid
for my ticket. We saw the latest American romance. The film was
touching. I fancy American movies—they have a pretty way of talking about love. I adore romances, like *Romeo and Juliet*. Do you
know it? It's one of my favorites. I stay away from war movies
because they stir up nightmares. I prefer movies to soaps, although
when I watch Mexican or Indian TV series, I'm on the edge of my
seat. Anyway, the actors I love the best are Mexican. I'm crazy about
the weekly shows that follow the love lives of men and women from
faraway countries.

I had a boyfriend. It was a real romance. We broke up. Sadness didn't miss its chance: it made me cry, then let me be. A lot of
boys hang around wanting me to give up my love. I'm not ready
for that yet. I'm not sure if I could fall in love with a Hutu boy. In
Nyamata, there is zero risk of that since we all know each other. I
know the boys from Gatare and the ones I socialize with in various activities. Even on the main street, we know where everyone
comes from, and it's a sharp line that keeps love away. At university, there are loads of young people, so things can be different. In

the huge city of Kigali, too, you interact with boys without knowing anything about their families. We talk, we joke around, we enjoy each other's company. Under no circumstances do we ask direct questions. There are Hutus who are tall and slim like Tutsis and seem equally polished and polite, except when they disagree. When they seem to get along well with others, there is no way to identify them, so love could take advantage and sneak its way in. If I discovered that my sweetheart was Hutu, that would shake me up. But I don't think I could leave him. How do you know?

I have too many friends to count. Most are boys and girls I met at elementary school in Gatare. My best friends are those I palled around with at Maranyundo Girls School. That's the American middle school where I completed my compulsory subjects. I am now in my last year at Stella Matutina public high school, not far from Kigali. I am doing the physics-chemistry-mathematics combination, but I don't see myself studying science later. The nervous disorder, which I've had ever since the genocide, as you know, affects my concentration.

Nowadays I see my close girlfriends during vacations. We have fun talking at one or another of their houses. We take a seat on a bench or go for a stroll. We're happy without even trying. We can hardly wait to tell each other private, funny things. We fill one another in on the latest gossip and share popular videos. We meet up for church activities like choir. With certain girlfriends, sports are the thing. My long legs have encouraged me to continue playing basketball, and my classmates push me, too. I have a real knack for shooting the ball.

Me, I'm passionate about dance. It's an enchantment. I began as a little girl at church, and it always got me noticed. Dance is especially rewarding given my illness. At school, I lead the dance group. I also dance at the parish. When friends have a birthday, we all invite each other to dance; the fun takes our breath away. I perform traditional Rwandan dance very, very beautifully. It's the *imbyino* rhythm of the drums. I dance publicly wearing amazing dresses at ceremonies like marriages and baptisms. In Nyamata, the district's troupe tried to recruit me, but my mama didn't want me going on long-distance tours. When I finish school, I hope to join a famous company—and why not visit faraway lands?

My friends and I are really keen on the internet. We meet up in Nyamata's cybercafés, we surf the web together, and I fool around on my Facebook page. A lot of people I know have sent me friend requests; we become better friends as we message more, especially the girls. I also get ordinary messages. I chat with my brother, Bertrand, because he is studying at an American university. I play games, too. I exchange news with my friend Kate, who was a teacher at Maranyundo Girls School. Pictures spring up from all over. We sing their praises for fun. My friends and I watch music videos on YouTube. We sift through singers' personal lives and compare notes, but not as frequently as young people in America do. We sometimes joke around on Skype. My mama gave me a smartphone, which she keeps tabs on with her stern voice because charges can soar without warning. We also surf the web at school. They allow us an hour a week to do our research on Google and the like. With a little pocket money, you can buy two hours of browsing on the weekends, but no more, because the classmates in line behind you get annoyed.

I avoid browsing sites that show how topsy-turvy the world is. The vicious AIDS epidemic that has devastated so many lives, people killing one another all over the world, the flooding from tsunamis, acts of terrorism—it's all pretty frightening. Myself, I think the speed of the internet and the like has a hand in the misfortunes. Young people take pleasure in sex videos, they marvel at the debauchery of the rich, and they believe the rumors spread by cults. I imagine that God is a bit jealous. He doesn't appreciate being pitted against the fame and money here on earth. He is violently forcing us to return to His path. Luckily, the madness of technology hasn't spread in Rwanda as much as it has elsewhere. We still devote ourselves to our faith without getting distracted by philosophical ideas that celebrate materialism.

I'm a happy Catholic. We are a devout and cheerful family, my mama, my brother, and I. My brother prays with all his heart in America. At my school, the nuns are overly strict in applying the rules; the prayer bells ring three times a day at specific times. But at home, prayers come in their own time whenever the mood takes you. I grew up with the joy of singing and prayer. At church, I sing in a choir, I dance during religious holidays. I'm involved in classes that explain the Gospels to uneducated people. The calm of Catholicism makes me glad. Catholics spend more time in communion than other believers. I admire the splendor of the faith: the icons move me deeply, as do the vestments of the priests, and the statues fill me with nostalgia. I know that in Europe young people boast about their disregard for religion. They consider their lives comfortable enough that they don't have to believe; they think they have nothing more to gain but constraints. They find it funny to waste one's time on faith. They delight in provocation. In reality, they are never satisfied; what they lack is always one step ahead of them. They suffer because of their indifference.

I grew up in a family steeped in the word of God. I know that God is everywhere. My papa was killed by the soldiers of the genocide because his time had come. I know that God was there, very much alive. He didn't forget my papa. He invited him gladly into His kingdom because He forgets no one. Then He breathed strength into the *inkotanyi* in time for them to save those who were meant to be saved.* I know that God saved my mama, my brother, and me for mysterious reasons. Not luck, or bravery, or virtue—it was God. Mama showed remarkable courage during those weeks of machetes, and Papa just as much with a man's strength. Yet God took him from us. No one knows how to interpret that.

I understand people who struggle to keep faith in God after the attempt to exterminate the Tutsis. Each of us believes and thinks according to our own history. If people have seen their loved ones savagely cut down, if no comforting voices are left to teach them the Holy Scriptures, if they have no one to inspire trust in God in them again, it's perfectly normal for them to want to turn their back on everything. Myself, I was lucky to be introduced to God by my mama, although she herself lost almost her entire family.

Thanks to her, I hold out hope that the culprits didn't wield their machetes in cold blood, without madness, but that they were driven by a diabolic force. I believe that Satan's cynicism was behind the machetes. I fear his tricks. Nonetheless, I still have my faith in human beings. It keeps me from stumbling when I'm shaken on my path by memories of my papa and my grandparents. Or when Mama's grief overcomes me. My mama guides me through. She talks a lot about forgiveness, but not just any kind of forgiveness. She doesn't pardon hastily. She obeys God, not some earthly authority. That was the good fortune I grew up with. My mama's faith breathed joy into our house.

MY NAME IS Sandra Isimbi. It means "precious one," like a precious stone. My mama's name is Édith Uwanyiligira. She works

---

*Inkotanyi, meaning "invincibles," is the name given to the Tutsi-led RPF rebels.

in administration at the secondary school. My brother's name is Bertrand, and he is currently studying on a campus in America, as I told you. My papa was killed in the Kabgayi region. We still don't know how. It was May 29. The soldiers arrived in the court-yard where we had holed up. They found him in his hiding place and took him away.

We were living in a house in Ntarama in April 1994. As soon as the killers began their expeditions on the hill, we and many others took refuge in the marshes. My papa stood his ground along with a group of young men. Because he was a well-known teacher and the captain of the Nyamata soccer team, they followed him without batting an eye. The Hutus attacked them every day in greater and more deadly numbers. Finally, my papa decided to make for Kabgayi to hide his family with a younger brother at the Electrogas plant. We zigzagged through the bush and crossed the river. We slept under trees, we ate what we picked, and we drank the water on the leaves. Papa carried two-year-old Bertrand. Me, I traveled on Mama's back because I was a five-month-old baby.

My mama told me the story. Once in Kabgayi, we lasted for several days in different hiding spots while the killings dragged on elsewhere. My mama was betrayed the first time by a neighbor woman, but without dire consequences because we managed to escape. The second time was fatal. The authorities showed boundless determination in their search for my papa. After they pushed him into a bus along with the other unlucky men, they tried to catch my mama. They were overzealous. The bus left. We never saw or heard anything more about my papa. No one ever came to our place with information. During the *gaçaças*, not one witness offered the smallest detail for us even to imagine what had happened. I have no interest in going back to help myself visualize the spot where they caught him. What good would it do? I don't know where they took him.

Every year on May 29, our family tries to go through what happened. It's painful not to know anything. Whenever we hear that a family is digging up a loved one's bones found in some remote place and that they are burying him with Christian care, I can see how moved Mama is by the ceremony. I know that she talks to herself about it every night before sleep overtakes her. She often says that the mystery of her husband's death is what eats away at her the most. The despair never leaves her.

When I was a little girl, I knew that my papa wasn't at home, I mean, I knew that he had been killed during the genocide. It wasn't something I thought about very much. In all honesty, I avoided it. Occasionally, I heard stories about the killings at home. They were startling and faraway. Mama would answer questions about the death of her loved ones. She seemed willing: she showed no signs of sadness; she didn't dwell. Visitors and friends shared their misfortunes. My brother, Bertrand, and I could hear them. But after having seen the terrifying films on television, I didn't hang around to listen to their conversations. Basically, I was satisfied with simple questions about my papa, and my mama would tell me.

I was eleven years old, I think, when I had my revelation about the genocide. How? I don't remember now. I think that one day I pricked up my ears to what was being said. Mama was giving details and descriptions of the killings to some people stopping by. I couldn't understand. It rattled around in my brain—imagining neighbors running after us Tutsis, machetes in their hands. Can a child even grasp it at first? I thought the words were only meant to strike fear in us—I mean, to punish the ears of the disobedient children who secretly listened in.

I told Mama my worries. Her expression was calm. She said, "The time has come to speak to you directly." She explained how the expeditions unfolded, how the people were cut, how the corpses took the place of the living in the dark water and in the thickets. She later told me about our family, about the muddy marshes below Ntarama, our frantic escape through the bush to Kabgayi, as I said, and the wandering without end or hope along the paths back to Ntarama. She told me about her lost relatives. I went with her to the edge of the marshes. She was very distraught. Since she didn't want us to see her like that, she stayed silent to save us the shock. With a group of survivors or at the parish, she could grieve with flowing tears. In front of her children, she hid her aching heart.

I HAVE A trusted friend—we're very close. She is a survivor, obviously. She mourns her papa and her grandparents, like me. Her mama has remarried. The FARG helps her shoulder the cost of school. The two of us talk about the genocide, but we never exaggerate our misfortunes, because plenty of young people suffer more than us from loneliness. A lot of them lead grueling lives in the fields. My friend comes from a different region. We tell each other our feelings as well as our thoughts. We share a survivor's past but one without personal memories—we were too little. We try to imagine ourselves at the time, how things must have been for us, what our families lived through. Often, though, we forget all that and discuss the happy surprises of the present. The circle of flirty boys, whom we rate and make fun of. Then something comes up that pushes us to continue our survivors' talk. Basically, we help each other avoid harmful bouts of loneliness.

I am active in associations of young survivors. At school, there are a dozen of us, all with FARG scholarships, who make up a local branch. It's a school for girls from well-to-do families where we don't have the right to mention our ethnicity. We meet without anyone knowing. The school officials have expressed their disapproval, especially when the FARG has been late with our *miner-*

vals. They sound off indignantly in front of everyone, and the other students are quick to chime in. That stings. Some students reproach us for being given special treatment because of the FARG. They say, "You girls, you don't have to worry about your exams because they'll pay the *minervals* no matter what, even if you don't get good grades." And we tell them, "You're absolutely right. If you'd had the good fortune of seeing your father cut before your very own eyes, you wouldn't be worried about grades or anything else."

Me, I'm happy to be helped by the FARG. I don't feel embarrassed by it. The nasty things certain schoolmates say still vex me, though. I know survivor children saddled with grief who have to work the fields; they don't receive any aid because they were born just after the killings. They stumble through life because their families have lost faith in everything. I have accepted being a survivor. It doesn't bother me. Day after day I should have died under the machete. Even if I wasn't fully conscious of it at five months old, I still feel very much like a survivor since, miraculously, I came out alive. The mean words people say sometimes tear me apart, or certain words give me a start. I'm not the only one. Which is why young Tutsis like us share our experiences with one another. We discuss witness accounts we have heard, and we help each other in order to raise survivors' hopes.

I know only the stories about the Tutsis that my mama has told me. Long ago, they were noble and tall, wise, with good manners, even when poor. They lived surrounded by cow herds. They gave freely, they were quite considerate and generous—among one another, anyway. The Hutus showed themselves to be farmers of incredible strength, capable of amazing feats. They would fertilize their fields and sow them in a single day. They have always envied the Tutsis' cattle, which, on top of that, do damage by trampling on their crops. Hutus don't see how they can trust Tutsis, and

Tutsis feel the same way. When Hutus disagree with Tutsis, they don't offer an explanation, they growl grumbling words.

Those who steeped their hands in blood can no longer flaunt their strength in the same way. Their faces have become mean and suspicious. I have noticed it in people who come back from prison. I am talking about the ones who plied the machete, not about their children or wives. The ex-prisoners cast nasty looks at us, as if they were still blaming the survivors for not being dead instead of blaming themselves for what they did. I don't panic at the sight of machetes; nothing dangerous is in store. And yet I'm afraid of those nasty looks in a way that I can't explain. Obviously, children of the killers sometimes try to be nice. They don't look at us as their parents do because they never raised the machete. Can they imagine what we lived through? I don't think so.

FOR A YOUNG PERSON, you're better off being born in a family of survivors, since so many young Hutus have been contaminated by their parents' actions. They grow up with shame or bad thoughts. Myself, I grew up without my papa. Sadness didn't forget me. But good fortune decided that I would be surrounded by the love of my mama, Édith, and Bertrand. I am cradled with kindness, buoyed by the presence of friends. I don't feel ashamed of anything, neither of my father's death nor of my illness. I am loved; nothing bad weighs on me, like resentment or remorse. But poor young Hutus grow up without the affectionate arms of a peaceful family. Why can't they overcome the obstacles? They lead an unhealthy existence, troubled by wary looks and silences. Some have lost their papas in prison or in Congo from malaria without a soul to comfort them.

I know a classmate from primary school whose papa is still in Rilima. He jumps whenever the genocide is mentioned, out of fear that someone will bring up his papa. Even though his skinny little boy's legs weren't even strong enough to hold him at the time, he still feels tainted today. He is constantly saying that, despite his regular visits to his papa in prison, he wants to be at the forefront of Rwanda's rebuilding. He is the only young Hutu who is willing to talk.

Other Hutus are as ashamed as he is, and as silent. It is impossible to know what they keep hidden. They never show themselves vulnerable, and they don't want to take comfort or to give it. Then there are those who go along with their parents, especially if their papa is living in prison. They fear making his time there worse. I have a schoolmate whose papa turns out to have been a notorious ringleader during the genocide. He refuses to criticize him. He has chosen family loyalty over his parents' disapproval.

I can't imagine Hutu family life at all. I have never eaten with a Hutu family. It must be degrading to talk about all this with them. What kind of person is going to tell their children stories about the hunts through the swamps over an evening meal? I have never heard a young Hutu get angry about what his parents tell him. Hutus feel too intimidated to come up to a girl like me, someone whose papa was killed, to share their anxieties. The ones who make a show of doubting the genocide watch the truth go by as if it were a movie. They don't find it shocking. The only thing that disturbs them is their own poverty.

Genocide is now my country's history. I have a passion for telling and hearing about it. Not every week, but when the opportunity arises. Plus, people who are sympathetic sometimes do you a good turn for telling them about it—they offer little rewards. I like to state my opinions as a survivor, especially in front of young Hutus. Even if our discussions don't go back and forth, I make sure they know what I lost because of their parents' crimes. I'm not embarrassed to say what we have been through. I teach them a lesson so that they never take pride in any of it. When a group of people has seen itself almost exterminated, it never feels out of harm's way. Some criminals have brought back a wickedness from prison like the one they took with them when they went in. Watch out: don't listen to people who claim that the page is turned. Too many ex-killers out there are merely faking it. Human beings never shake off the experience of living like animals.

I would sincerely like to forgive them for the harm they caused us. I would like to. It's all mixed up in my heart. As a child, there were times when I couldn't handle living alongside Hutus. As soon as I thought about my papa, hate tightened its grip. I buried it deep inside me. That was melancholy. I thought only about revenge, I imagined the details. I felt humiliated. I thought about the faces of the people I love, about their trust betrayed, about my own face, the gaze of a young happy girl, of a Christian. In other words, these kinds of bad thoughts brought me low. Time is a good preacher. My mama has encouraged in me the example of the Bible's forgiveness, and I try hard to follow a peaceful path.

Simply put, those are the events of my childhood.

ERNESTINE'S MURDER

IT HAPPENS ON FRIDAY, APRIL 15, AT THE CHURCH in Ntarama, in the middle of a eucalyptus forest. From the moment the radio announces President Juvénal Habyarimana's assassination, Tutsi families from the nearest hills—Kibungo, Nyarunazi, and Kanzenze—rush to take refuge inside the church enclosure, for, with each pogrom over the past fifty years, they have continued to believe that they would find protection within the walls of God.

At around eleven o'clock in the morning, whatever illusions they have vanish along with the men escaping into the forest and bush, men too poorly armed to defend themselves against those making their way up the hill: a column of soldiers and *interahamwe* ahead of a horde of farmers, brandishing machetes, axes, spades, and all sorts of other implements. The farmers have been brought by truck from Nyamata, about twenty kilometers away, or led on foot from their fields through the woods. The soldiers use grenades to breach the walls of the church courtyard. They surge forward weapons-first, hurling themselves on the families huddled in the grass. Then they storm inside. They cut down anything that moves: the elderly, women, and the children whose mothers haven't already left them behind. They hack until their arms ache, transforming over the next few hours a mass of people into heaps of corpses. When they finally withdraw in the afternoon, the killers leave in their wake about five thousand dead and several hundred dying, whom they return to finish off at the same time the following day. Some people survive, most often shielded from the blades by the corpses fallen on top of them.

Among the survivors is Janvier Munyaneza, a nine-year-old boy who remembered the slaughter in *Life Laid Bare*: "All we could hear was the commotion of the attacks. We were almost paralyzed amid the machetes. People were almost dead before the fatal blow. My first sister asked a Hutu she recognized to kill her without making her suffer. He said yes, pulled her out by the arm onto the grass, and struck her with his club. Then a close neighbor, named Habyarimana, shouted that she was pregnant. He sliced open her belly with a stroke of his knife. I weaved my way through the corpses, but unfortunately a boy managed to hit me with his bar. I fell flat on top of the corpses. I didn't budge. I made my eyes dead."

For sixteen years, the brutality of the murder of his sister, Ernestine Kaneza, was lost beneath the memory of five thousand corpses. Then came the *gaçaça* trials. During one of the hearings, held beneath the branches of an acacia tree not far from the church, a young soldier asked permission to speak. It was Janvier. He had come home on leave from the Kivu region. He wanted to testify.

Before we hear his account, let us return to those first days of the genocide on the Ntarama hill, turning to the more detailed recollections of his brother Vincent, who, three years his senior, farms the family plot on a hillside in Kiganwa. He recalls: "It was during the April school vacation. A cowherd and I were leading the cows to pasture when his eldest brother came shouting, 'We absolutely have to leave. The Hutus have started killing in

Kanzenze.' We ran to the church, which is only a few kilometers away. We camped near the enclosure without going directly in so we could keep an eye on the cows. My mama decided to make a break for Kigali, taking the smallest children with her. I tried to catch them. Looking down from where we were, I could see the men hacking them with machetes on the bridge. I retraced my steps.

"On the fifteenth, the *interahamwe* arrived singing. They smashed open the doors of the church. I had the speedy legs of someone used to chasing after cows. I raced down to the marshes behind my papa, my oldest brother, and many other men. Janvier's short legs kept him from coming with us. He stayed with his two sisters in the church. That night, those of us who had survived the marshes went back up to the church to save anyone who could still be saved. It was my papa who dragged Janvier out from under the corpses. He seemed dazed, but he was still alive. He somehow found the words to tell us how our sister Ernestine had been taken out of the church by Vincent Habyarimana and Modeste Mfizi. He called them by name, without hesitation, because both men were our close neighbors in Kiganwa. My papa examined the corpses behind the church. He found Ernestine sliced open from her genitals to chin, with the baby scattered in pieces next to her. It was only during the *gaçaças* that we learned the sad fate of my other sister, Christine Mukaruhogo. How she was taken away by the mob of killers to the Kibungo town square, stripped naked, and macheted to the howls and jeers of a huge crowd."

According to Vincent's account, a group of seven friends participated in the killing of April 15, including Vincent Habyarimana, Modeste Mfizi, Emmanuel Bampoliki, and Fulgence Bunani. The latter ordinarily worked with his gang of Adalbert, Pio, Pancrace, and Alphonse—with whom I wrote *Machete Season*—but on that day he threw in with some others whom he had met along the way. We already know what happened next. Janvier, Vincent, and their father survived hidden in the papyrus of the Cyugaro marshes. The killers fled with their families to the Kivu region in eastern Congo, where they settled in a camp for two years. In 1996, troops from the RPF led them back to Rwanda by force.* Upon their return, most were imprisoned at the penitentiary in Rilima, where they were tried for the first time. Ernestine's father didn't testify, having died from exhaustion prior to the trials, nor did his sons, who were still too young. That explains why the murder wasn't mentioned at the time. The seven men received prison terms of about fifteen years apiece, all except Habyarimana, who was sentenced to life for his role as one of the ringleaders of the expeditions.

Seven years later, in 2003, all except Habyarimana benefited from an amnesty law and returned to their land. Fulgence reunited with his wife, Jacqueline Mukamana, and his two sons, Idelphonse and Jean-Damascène. He was a tireless farmer. At daybreak every morning he headed out, hoe in hand, to his field near the river. He built a larger house to make room for the arrival of new children and started distilling *urwagwa* again. He found his way back to church and to the cabaret in Nyarunazi, where he would share a bottle with his accomplices Pancrace, Pio, and others, like Ignace.

When the *gaçaça* court opened on his hill, Fulgence wasn't overly concerned by his many summonses to appear beneath the tall tree. At each hearing he kept to the tacit arrangement offered by the authorities: that the accused who cooperated and admitted to crimes would leave just as free as they had arrived. Neither he nor anyone else had anticipated that, one fine morning in Rilima

---

*The Rwandan Patriotic Front (RPF) is a Tutsi organization formed in 1987 in Uganda; it carried out its first military operations in 1990, which led to the death of its founder, Fred Rwigema. On the first day of the genocide, the RPF launched a major offensive into Rwanda, taking control of the country on July 4, 1994, under the command of Paul Kagame, the strong man of the Republic.

prison, Habyarimana would ask to testify in the hope of seeing his sentence reduced. That was when Janvier first heard of what was afoot and decided to join Habyarimana at the trial. He described the details of his sister Ernestine's murder and stated, "From where I was in the church, my eyes saw clear as day Habyarimana and Mfizi lead my sister outside."

A long silence fell over the proceedings. The *gaçaça*'s presiding judge, Célestin Mangazini, remembers it well: "We looked at each other, dumbstruck. No words came to our lips because of the details of the young woman's disembowelment. Then a terrible commotion took hold of the audience. Without further ado, we sentenced the two defendants to fifteen years."

No sooner had the ruling been delivered than Mfizi found himself back in prison with his accomplice, Habyarimana. Furious, Mfizi lodged an appeal in which he promised to reveal the whole truth of what had occurred. The authorities named a neutral *gaçaça* court in Musenyi, a hill thirty kilometers away. Emmanuel was called to appear under the acacia. He promptly denounced his six sidekicks and then, ever the sly one, took advantage of nightfall to slip away into the eucalyptus, after which he eventually escaped to Uganda.

The presiding judge immediately summoned the six other men. It was the first time that Fulgence's name had been mentioned in the case. Utterly unaware of what was transpiring at the *gaçaça*, Fulgence offered his swollen feet as an excuse to spend the Sunday quietly at home. He would have cause to regret it. In his absence, the *gaçaça* judge repeatedly called upon the men either to assume responsibility for the crime or to denounce the killer. Each denied his own involvement more adamantly than the next. The angry crowd grumbled.

As Célestin Mangazini recalls, "If they confessed, we weren't going to send them back to prison. Clemency had opened its arms to those who asked forgiveness. Pardons had been granted right and left. But they were too ashamed. In front of their neighbors' eyes, none of them could admit to having so brutally cut a young pregnant lady and her child. The culprits clung to their denials. Anger seized the judges and the public. They were shocked and outraged. The verdict rang out, and it was merciless: life in prison for them all. It was the last day of the *gaçaças*, the final decision of a supplementary session on a Sunday evening. It was the group's bad luck, if I may put it that way."

Five kilometers down the hill, on the stony path that leads to Kiganwa, Fulgence had little reason to suspect that his fate had just taken a very sour turn. His wife, Jacqueline, confirms as much: "It was dark outside, a Sunday, after supper. Customers were passing a bottle around in our cabaret, but Fulgence was already resting his feet in bed. Myself, I was cleaning utensils in the yard. He went out to pee. I heard the customers shouting. I went out, my little girl sticking close behind me. That's how she saw him, her child's eyes wide, staring at her papa tied up with rope. Three men pushed him along. I ran after them to put a jacket over his bare shoulders. I snuck the money from the evening's drink sales from his pocket. The night was especially dark, a Sunday with no way out. I feared that they might simply kill him on the way, which is why I sent the two boys to follow behind the little procession. Was Fulgence ignorant of what was happening at the *gaçaça*? Yes. He knew the group had been called, but the summons said he only needed to give testimony. He wasn't thinking of new charges. His feet had swollen—the pain shot up as high as his hips. He sent a boy to provide his excuse. And that's how they tied him up and dragged him off to Kibungo. At the *gaçaça*, the verdict had already been announced for quite some time; the van had already taken the judges off into the night. Nothing was left to say. He was jailed at the sector office. The next day a truck brought him to Rilima.

"Do I know if Fulgence took part in the killings? I would think so, since he went off with the expeditions like so many other men. But Ernestine's murder, that's a big thing. I remember the night of the killing, on the fifteenth. Who doesn't remember it? He came home with someone called Sylvère. They were sweating—they smelled of sweat through and through. They sat down, they didn't ask for anything to drink. They seemed somewhat traumatized. They were panicked by the bad things done. Fulgence put down his machete and said, 'What we saw today goes beyond anything so far. May God forgive me and help me not to go back!'

"If that was the day he became a butcher, wouldn't his wife have noticed in bed?"

JEAN-DAMASCÈNE NDAYAMBAJE

SIXTEEN YEARS OLD

Son of Fulgence Bunani, Hutu prisoner

THE RELEASE FROM PRISON IN 2003, THAT remarkable year, I remember. It was the dry season. A gentleman came and set down his bundle on the last step of a two-day journey. He gave hugs and kisses all around. He wasn't tall, but he wasn't short, either. We didn't see him as someone special. At first I thought that he was simply paying the family a visit, because I had no idea who he was. I had never been taken to Rilima, even though I was already seven years old. It was a tidy sum for a child to rent a bicycle. My mama told us that the man was our papa. She said that all the prisoners had been granted pardons and that we were going to live as a family again. My papa was given a warm welcome. His clothes weren't made of handsome fabric, his shoes had no laces. He sat down with us, he shared the bottle, and he spoke comforting words. He was glad just giving compliments, I think.

You could tell that his eyes were sorry to see the holes in the house's metal siding and the dry banana trees. He held back his reprimands. I was happy to know that he was my papa. Neighbors stood in line to greet him and, of course, to have a taste of drink for free. They stayed late to talk. Mama decided against killing a kid goat, so as not to appear proud in the neighbors' eyes. We still ate brochettes, and we tapped *urwagwa* from the jerry cans. It was the first celebration we had had in a very long time. Papa relaxed at home the whole day long without walking off to town. Mama was full of life and laughter. She was festive, and didn't skimp on the jugs of drink.

Papa and Mama took up their tools before sunrise and worked in the field until nightfall. They did the same the next day. Papa left every morning without saying a word. He uprooted the stumps of a seven-year-old jungle. He sowed tomato plants in the low valley, near the river. We were no longer accustomed to such fancy crops; we had gotten by with beans. It made us admire him. He built a picket fence for the small livestock, and he dug a watertight pit for the *urwagwa*. A normal family existence offered itself to us. Good fortune stopped turning its back. Papa set about building a new house, he added a brick veranda, he opened a drink business. People congratulated him.

Then, at seven years old, I was given my first schoolbag. There was no more teasing on the walk to school—no Tutsi kids went that way anymore. Each year I climbed straight into the next grade. The teacher was strict with everyone. I enjoyed learning. My exams ranked me at the top of the class, where I really excelled. I showed off in ball games with classmates. Soccer was my joy. In the evenings, I fetched water from the river, like so many others, and I cut feed for our animals. At that age, you don't yet raise the hoe.

Our plot gave in abundance, and the banana grove grew strong. We cleared fertile land along the marshes and harvested beans in quantities large enough to sell. Two mother sows added to the pig farm. Many neighbors came to sit on the veranda to drink our banana beer. You could see that they liked the taste. We got used to the good life again. I sometimes went with my papa to the Nyamata market, where we could sell at better prices. On Sundays, we walked as a family to our church in Kibungo. At mass, Papa often presided as God's servant—they dressed him in a white chasuble, just like before the genocide. After the service, everyone broke into groups of acquaintances. If a soccer game was starting, I hurried off to the field. I loved nothing better than soccer. I sometimes got to watch televised games in downtown Nyarunazi. Me, I root for Real Madrid. I don't know why—the team just makes me happy.

Papa lasted for seven years at home. He described the journey to Congo and life in prison. I didn't ask him questions. I never asked him why. No, not a single question about the killings. I felt too little to ask him personal questions about his bad behavior. The traditional respect a child has for his papa is the same as trepidation. No questions for my mama, either, because she was blessed to be busy by her husband's side. And none for my older brother, Idelphonse, for fear of being scolded.

Papa's freedom made me glad, and I thanked God for it. On the hill, there were plenty of good friends whose papas had been released in the same line of prisoners. We talked about it among ourselves. We said that our papas had had a hand in the genocide and that they had truly confessed their mistakes. We counted ourselves lucky. We discussed the situation without singling out the details of any particular misdeeds. We didn't linger over rumors; we kept clear of them. We avoided them because deep down they made us uneasy.

Papa was sent back to prison in 2010. We were taken by surprise. It was a Sunday. Someone came looking for him to testify at the *gaçaça* court one last time. His swollen foot shot pain all the way up his thigh. I think he sent a messenger boy to present his excuse. He had already confessed to everything he was supposed to, so he wasn't on his guard. He had spoken as he should during his first trial and they rewarded him with amnesty. He spoke at the *gaçaças* seven years later, he added details, and they thought he did well. Then, the final day, he stayed home to rest his foot. That evening, the chief of the *mudugudu*, along with some tough-looking men, came to take him away. They tied him up and dragged him off to the sector jail, then to Rilima the following day. I was fourteen years old. It wasn't easy to understand what they might be accusing him of again. I could have asked for more information. Mama would have given me answers. I felt too confused by what was happening. I stayed out of it. I stopped school shortly afterward.

MY NAME: Jean-Damascène Ndayambaje. It means "pray to God." I was born in Congo in 1996. I don't know where. All I have been told is that that was where I came into the world. My father's name is Fulgence Bunani. He is a farmer and merchant. He has a *urwagwa* business, but he currently lives in the penitentiary. My mama's name is Jacqueline Mukamana. She farms our plot. I grew up in this house here in Kiganwa. I finished primary school in Kibungo, always at the top of the class. I was supposed to start secondary school in Kanzenze when my papa was sent back behind the high walls. I enrolled at the trade school in Nyamata. A humanitarian organization paid for tuition. Completing an apprenticeship can quickly prove its worth.

Me, I wanted to do auto mechanics. I was fond of engines and bodywork. Unfortunately, the organization didn't approve; they gave me a choice between hospitality and tailoring. I learned tailoring, I felt more drawn to fabrics than to cabarets. Finishing pants and vests is something I find satisfying. Even though I prefer engines, I like to sew beautiful cloth. The training ended in success. I had to provide my own sewing machine to get a spot in a tailor's shop—that's the custom. The humanitarian organization promised me a Singer. I waited, but nothing came, so that's how I ended up in my mama's footsteps, back on the family land.

I get up at 5:30 and immediately leave for the field. Do I eat some porridge? Not every day. The parcel is near the river, less than an hour trek. Mama and I work in harmony, doing what the seasons demand. My brother, Idelphonse, goes on his own to fish and doesn't take up the hoe until the afternoon. I come home at eleven o'clock to prepare the noon meal for the family. My mama takes care of it in the evening. I rest until three o'clock. I fetch water, gather firewood, then cut feed for the pigs. In the evenings, we eat, I can sell our drink to make a little money, or I take a walk in the neighborhood. If I am worn out from work, I go to bed earlier.

I don't go down to the parcel very often on the weekends, only when the rain requires it. Saturday mornings, it's laundry. I feed the animals so that I'm free in the afternoons. We fetch water, we have a meal. I go for a walk to visit friends—the children of neighboring farmers, former schoolmates, or people I like from church. We stroll around, we sit on a stone wall or in the shade of a tree if the sun is too hot, and we talk when we want. We catch up on unimportant news and crack jokes like people who haven't seen each other for a long time. I go to Nyarunazi, the local center. I hang around late at the market. We sometimes have the chance to watch television or share a Primus beer. I don't spend time in Nyamata. It's too far and too costly. I go there to sell if we have a good harvest, or an animal, because prices run higher than here.

I HEARD TALK about the killings from early on in my childhood. Papa already lived at the penitentiary. It was on everyone's lips. I heard memories in our cabaret. When men get drunk on

Primus, the killings stream into the stories that come flowing out. Especially when someone lets fly with piercing words.

At the time, I heard these low voices but didn't make much of them. I was too little to be interested in war and all that. Once, at the edge of the field, I heard farmworkers taking a break under a tree, day laborers from Ruhengeri. They started talking about Papa's misdeeds. I secretly pricked up my ears. They spoke of Papa but also of his colleagues and prison. They discussed how the Rwandans had risen up against each other. That evening, I asked Mama about it. She replied that Papa was being punished, since he was in prison. She couldn't find her way to a simple explanation why. In any case, it didn't excite my curiosity. In Kiganwa, almost all the papas were in prison—not a single word was said against them. We children waited; things went smoothly.

Then Papa left Rilima. He told us about the terrible flight to Congo, the confessions at the trial, and the presidential pardon. He never tired of talking about God. He explained the evil tricks that Satan plays on people. As I said, I was too little to ask questions. Basically, I heard about it like a story whose details are too frightening to want to know. Have I visited the marshes? We often go down there to farm the wet silt during the dry season or to gather grass for the *urwagwa*. We never discuss the expeditions. It isn't something we think about.

I have a good friend whom I trust named Twisimane. He lives next door, and his papa wore the pink prisoner's uniform. We understand each other; we talk about life on the hill. We listen to "hype music" on his radio because we don't have internet. We don't go dancing with girls because there are no places to dance, except in Nyamata. We sometimes mix with the boys and girls our age. Do we mention the killings of '94? No, or if we do, only by accident. We don't see any good from discussing them, except to complain about Papa's absence or the hardships of poverty. With the Tutsis I know, I haven't been willing to bring them up. We get along by avoiding all that.

I gave up the classroom. When I earn a little money from the *urwagwa*, it isn't enough for fun in Nyamata. I don't come across survivor families in Kiganwa. In Nyarunazi or in Kibungo, nothing intimate is shared between ethnicities. I think the young people on both sides have suffered. We have faced painful obstacles. Nothing from '94 has fallen down the memory hole. No chance of slipping away from it. Young Tutsis think of those they have lost. The teachers lecture them to consider forgiveness. Young Hutus think of what they have lost, too; they have to appear humble and compassionate. Out of convenience, we steer clear of each other.

I HAVE NEVER spoken with Ernestine's brothers. I'm too young to approach them. Would I even find a word to say? They might want to show me how angry they are. I leave it in the hands of silence. Obviously, the situation upsets me. Do I know if my papa's punishment is fair? I don't know enough of the details, except for what people say. Before, I was intimidated, and I didn't ask Papa a single question. Now that age has whet my curiosity, Papa has been taken away again and I don't have the opportunity to question him anymore.

Asking Mama might hurt her feelings. Women aren't made like men for those kinds of killings; they don't raise the machete. They stew over their sorrows more than men and fall silent. If Papa leaves Rilima, I plan to ask him questions. I hope that he provides answers that a son can accept, otherwise it will be harmful and make me unhappy. That's understandable, isn't it? Before, I was fine with what I heard at school. Now that people gossip about Ernestine's murder, I have to glean information about my family. My dreams fill me with panic at night. Terrible visions pass before my eyes. Like what? Men hurtling through the bush, a bloody brawl inside a church. When I wake up, I reel off prayers without the time to catch my breath. I beg God to protect my loved ones against illness. I plead for my papa's freedom and for reconciliation between neighbors. A genocide stirs religious belief: people rouse their faith to protect themselves from disaster.

THE PARENTS

MOTHER COURAGE

WHEN I INVITE HER FOR OUR FIRST MEETING, AT A restaurant at the bus station, Jacqueline Mukamana orders a chicken served with fried bananas and one or two Primus beers. With her elegant fingers, she meticulously savors the meal, especially since she also feeds little bites of it to her baby, leaving behind only a licked-clean carcass on her plate. When we meet a second time, at the Coin des amis in Kanzenze, she makes do with half a chicken, taking the other half home in a doggy bag, having coaxed the last drop of beer from the bottles left on the table. This is because, since her husband's return to Kilima, the Bunani family has had to go without meat and beer. Although destitution has yet to befall them, it is knocking at their door.

Jacqueline lives in Kiganwa, near Kibungo. We take the route from Kanzenze, then turn right onto a road so rocky and broken that not a single bicycle ventures the climb. The road follows a ridge overlooking two deep valleys to the right and the left, each the paradise of myriads of songbirds. One valley rushes steeply down to the motionless river below; the second slopes gently toward other, smaller valleys, graced with the colors of the bush and the banana groves, through which shepherds lead their herds.

Kiganwa includes about fifty earth-and-sheet-metal houses, among which are a grocery store and a cabaret. The latter belongs to Jacqueline.

Every morning at dawn, as the drowsy family emerges into the courtyard, as women begin to bustle around the stove, as young girls wash up with the hose before donning their school uniforms, Jacqueline leaves the house. Wearing a muddy *pagne*, a T-shirt donated by an NGO, and a scarf wrapped tightly around her hair, she carries her tools over her shoulder. Her son Jean-Damascène picks up his tools and catches up with her. Joining a stream of neighbors, they take the river path that snakes toward the field. Their land, a bright ocher in the fresh morning light, is plowed, cleared of scrub, and carefully lined with furrows. It seems a huge expanse for only two pairs of arms, which, none too brawny to begin with, are away at the market on Wednesdays, at church on Sundays, and in Rilima on visiting days. Because of their absences, the mother and son have fallen behind, as can be seen with a quick glance at the neighboring fields, where rows of seedlings are already staked. In the banana grove, broken branches dangle, exhausted trees still need to be replaced, and a layer of gray leaves suffocates the soil.

Jacqueline attacks the earth with a hoe. If all goes well, they will have planted the beans a few days ahead of the first rains. Jean-Damascène looks up at the sky, whose pale-blue hue can only mean a scorching heat to come. He hesitates, then reaches for the hoe again. A hole, three seeds, a hole, three seeds, along a hundred-yard furrow at the end of which they stop just long enough to mop their brows before setting off in the other direction. No words are exchanged between them, no breath wasted under the burning sun. At morning's end, they walk one after the other back up the hill. With barely time to tidy up, they prepare the noon meal, the fodder for the pigs, and, of course, the jerry can of *urwagwa* to sell.

Jacqueline doesn't always find a few minutes to doze off in her hot bedroom; more often than not, she is back at work on the parcel by early afternoon.

The evening sun has already reddened the mountain ridge when she appears on the veranda to serve her drink. She wears a magnificent multicolor dress. She undoubtedly likes the flashy colors. The drinkers squeeze together on the benches. Candles are lit and jerry cans unstopped. The bottles are emptied and refilled; the *chalumeau* is passed around until late into the night. The men chat heartily as the family eats its evening meal in the courtyard behind them.

Of the twenty years since the genocide, Jacqueline has spent seven with her husband on their parcel and the others in the Kivu camp or at their home as a prisoner's wife. In Rilima, Fulgence cheers her with his advice, but it comes at the price of exhausting journeys to the penitentiary, expensive visits to the prison commissary, and attorney's fees for filing appeals. Unlike Marie-Chantal, Joseph-Désiré's wife, Jacqueline, never complains. She will never be seen asking for aid or charity. Apart from the feeling of injustice that has haunted her since Fulgence's last indictment, she never shows anger or resentment over these trouble-filled years. Unlike Consolée, she neither blames nor criticizes her husband for what he has subjected them to. Does she lack the nerve? Deep down, what does she really think? How complicit was she, if she was complicit? Ever welcoming, cheerful, and discreet, she is impossible to read. She is a strangely courageous mother, resistant to hardship, stalwart in raising her family, loyal, mute, and stubborn through adversity. The dignity with which she accepts her fate is nothing short of moving.

Following their return from Congo to Kiganwa, an area mainly populated by Hutus, at least one man in every family ended up in prison. The years passed, the men were released and found their way back to the fields and the cabarets. Ernestine's murder hit Jacqueline like a whirlwind that seems only to have devastated her parcel of land. Not a single customer has deserted her veranda, not a single insulting remark is made, but this time there is no one around to lend her a hand in the field or in the offices of the court authorities. The two boys are in the throes of adolescence, the little girl is at the age of persistent unanswered questions. It is a lonely time.

JACQUELINE MUKAMANA

HUTU FARMER

Mother of Idelphonse and Jean-Damascène

I AM GLAD TO GO TO THE MARKET WHEN I HAVE chicken or bananas to sell. Wednesdays are better because goods sell fast and we deal for higher prices. I meet old friends. As a woman without her husband, I can't enter the cabaret for a Primus. We have a nice chat outside. What I make at the market I bring to Rilima the next day.

Visits are once or twice a month. My son takes me on his bicycle, or I rent a bike-taxi for the day. The ride lasts four hours. When I arrive, I buy things for my husband at the prison commissary, especially sugar, fritters, and milk. Then I squeeze in line. When Fulgence comes out, we exchange news. We talk about the worries of the parcel, which are never in short supply. That lasts five minutes.

The children's education suffers because of Fulgence's imprisonment. I struggle as well. Their papa's authority is sorely missed, because children don't respect a woman as much as a man. The boys always see themselves as stronger, even at a young age. They only fear their papa. My eldest son, Idelphonse, has become rebellious. We quarrel; we don't understand each another. He no longer helps me hoe or sow the land. He goes off fishing in the evenings. If he traps a ten-kilo fish, he gets eight to ten thousand and drinks it all away. He buys himself Primus—he leaves nothing for his family, and he doesn't think about his child.

The small house next door to ours? His little brother and I are building it with our own two hands. Idelphonse hasn't picked up a single brick; he looks on and couldn't care less. Since Fulgence returned to prison, Idelphonse has taken to drinking. He suddenly thought that he was the boss, that everything belonged to him, that he should be issuing orders. I don't talk about it with Fulgence, so as not to make his situation worse. A son who lacks respect for his mother—Fulgence would bristle with anger. I keep quiet, but I feel responsible for the children. I try to show myself humble with the eldest son. I suffer in silence and I compensate with prayer. The two boys don't quarrel; they avoid each other. Jean-Damascène stays to rest at home while the oldest hangs around in the cabarets. They don't take the time to talk to each other. Each has his own way of thinking.

Sometimes Jean-Damascène says that he regrets not going back to school. He is fond of studying. That's the truth. He thinks that diplomas alone can ease his worries. He sees his salvation slipping away. But he still gladly lends me a hand with all the work. He follows me down to the parcel in the mornings, hoe in hand. He takes part in the house chores without a fuss. He buys sorghum to distill the *urwagwa*. He sells the drink to the neighbors and shares the money.

IT BOTHERED ME that Fulgence had a hand in the killings. When we came back from Congo, the dirty looks followed me on the roads of Nyarunazi and sometimes all the way to Nyamata. What else can I say? Does a wife speak against her husband? I don't know exactly how he got his machete mixed up in the expeditions, since the wives were supposed to keep quiet at home. He followed his peers with good cheer, everyone knows it, and they put him in prison for seven years. I have never heard the boys grumble about their papa. They learned that he wasn't the only one to get his blade wet. They didn't ask me how serious the suspicions were. But Idelphonse knew the details. Everyone talked about it. On our hill, only the dead avoided prison. When the men weren't hurling accusations at one another at the cabaret, they went in for mockery instead. The wives jabbered. The children picked up on the rumors, and they shared their thoughts on the sly. Idelphonse, despite his young age, brought home plenty of gossip from the cabaret. He never failed to tell Jean-Damascène. Myself, to try to reassure them, I told them, "Walk straight ahead and don't listen to the hateful words. Be brave. You children, you can visit your papa at the penitentiary. He hasn't been killed, his health is strong, he has advice to give. That's extraordinary luck that not all children have."

Fulgence admitted his misdeeds like so many others, and the judge sentenced him harshly. Twelve years in prison is a big thing. Then he received the presidential pardon. After his release in January 2003, he brought the children together and explained the consequences of the war. How the flames were fanned, the way people killed one another, why so many Tutsis perished in the papyrus without proper burials. Why the Hutus had to race to escape to Congo.

But certain truths are harmful in our situation. Words must be doubly cautious for children's ears. When you reveal too many details to a child who goes on to repeat them, they can turn into very serious accusations. An adolescent understands why secrets must be kept. A little child has no idea; he is liable to start talking about unimaginable crimes. It's scary. Me, I told them about the poverty in the camps, the plastic-sheet tents we lived in, how

Idelphonse was born in a completely unhealthy place. Fear tested the children. They prayed for those things never to happen again. Little by little, our anxieties left us. Fulgence and I cleared the land. We brought a boy and a girl into the world. It was twice the joy. Misfortune began to forget us. We expanded the parcel to the wet edge of the marsh and took up raising livestock, like the Tutsis. The *urwagwa* business prospered. We stopped thinking about the past.

Then the *gaçaça* courts came. We trembled like everyone else. Fulgence wanted the judges to see that he was cooperative. His voice never grumbled. He answered questions straightforwardly, he repeated his confessions and added details, and he admitted his offense. Those who heard him appeared satisfied. Fulgence came away from the tree of judgment without being charged. No one hurled insults, no one jeered. No one imagined that Ernestine's little brother would come to speak about his sister.

Do I believe Fulgence capable of the horrible crimes committed against Ernestine? The wife in me answers no. Blood used to give him such a fright that he couldn't cut a goat without his hands trembling. So, to slice open the lady's belly with his blade—would he even have tried? As I told you, if he had become a butcher like the others at the Nyamata church, I would have noticed that night in our bedroom.

Children don't doubt like adults—they take what they hear. They can accept it. I don't know where their certainty lies. In Kiganwa, everyone rushed to judgment. The children were rattled—a new calamity had swept down upon them. They didn't ask questions, except for the little girl. She is only six years old but already the smartest. She is at the top of the class all by herself. She gets terribly angry with her schoolmates if they make fun of her papa. Every night in her dreams she sees him leaving prison; she talks in her sleep. She asks sophisticated questions.

The children were beginning to discuss things aloud when they learned that the man called Emmanuel, the colleague who testified against their papa, had fled to Uganda. They were shocked. How can you trust an accuser who hides? They are angry that Fulgence wasn't heard by the judges, that the other men from the group argued among themselves. They suspect that there were jealousies at work and unfair interpretations. Me, I say encouraging words, I promise them a positive outcome. What do I tell them? "If Fulgence was involved like they say, let his punishment serve as an example, but then they have to provide us with legitimate proof in exchange." It calms them down a bit.

Thanks to God, the children pray fervently for his release. Even the oldest one, who has taken to the bottle, isn't too distracted to pray. Misfortune has made them more faithful believers.

MAMA NEMA'S VERANDA

TONIGHT, SYLVÈRE IS THE FIRST TO CLIMB THE STEPS
of Mama Nema's veranda. He picks a white plastic chair facing the
hillside. He has just walked the entire length of main street from
his work at the district offices. Mama Nema comes out of her courtyard to swap neighborhood news with him as she lights the candles on the tables. She hands him an Amstel and takes advantage
of one last respite to return to her stove. The sun traces a pink
streak low in the sky, announcing its imminent plunge beneath the
horizon. Soon darkness will envelop the road—or is it a lane?
Who knows what to call this steep path that runs from the covered
market, along the soccer field, to the top of Kayumba hill. In any
case, the route's ruts and cracks, as much as its precipitous ascent,
discourage even small trucks from making the climb, all of them
except Chicago's van, of course, which nothing can keep away.

What a pleasure it is to chat with Sylvère before the evening
rush. His apocalyptic irony, whose humor sometimes tends to the
grotesque, had once shocked me as it does others. Fairly quickly,
however, I learned to read in his chronic skepticism a form of
benevolent dismay. The mixture derives, no doubt, from the dis-
illusionment of a Tutsi child, born in a hovel in Maranyundo,

whose school smarts early on caught the keen eyes of church re-
cruiters. A brilliant student, he was enlisted with his friend
Gonzalve to study theology at Swiss and Canadian universities,
where they were saved from the machetes. The two clergymen,
whose futures destined them for the elite, abandoned their religious
vocation immediately after the killings, returned to Rwanda, and
rolled up their sleeves amid the devastation of Nyamata. Sylvère
was in charge of a primary school when I first met him at Marie-
Louise's place. Today, he is one of the district's most influential
senior civil servants and a party executive, although he is still
his old self when he enters the cabaret, with the same blunt, and
slightly Jesuitical, sense of ridicule.

Just before nightfall, Dominique emerges onto the veranda,
staggering off the street at the end of a retiree's trying day in the
cabarets. Éphraïm arrives next, still sporting his boots after a
lightning-fast inspection of his land as he left the office. Gonzalve,
the very embodiment of calm, has just come from Bugesera's high
school. Emmanuel occasionally drops by. Chicago will roll in
much later, despite the risks to his truck on his breakneck drive
from Kigali. Innocent, moodier by day's end, comes to badger or
tease one or another of the men or to tell amusing stories, when
he hasn't opted instead for the solitude of a corner market closer
to home.

Their group was once called the "circle of intellectuals," at a
time when people no longer dared to think. Devastated, Nyamata
had few schools. An emergency administration operated out of
several rooms in the district office building. Doctor Georges
worked his miracles at the clinic, with its population of acqui-
escent patients. A handful of agricultural engineers and veterinarians still raced their motorcycles up and down the hills, to
Kanazi in the south, to Kanzenze in the north, and to Kibungo
or Kiganwa farther out in the west. They kept at it out of a sense

of dignity. In the evenings, they convened to drink until they could drink no more, setting the world to rights with a humor that lacked in the world around them. They first pitched camp in Marie-Louise's boutique. Among its piles of fabrics, basins, and flour sacks, they sipped their beers and enjoyed the not-so-maternal kindness of the establishment's owner.

When Marie-Louise closed her place down, having already married off several customers along the way, the group migrated to Kayumba, where they discovered a different sort of motherly warmth at Mama Mwangera's boutique, with its candlelit walls and dim fluorescent bulb. Tite went his own way, preferring the dive bars, particularly his wife's, at the main intersection nearer to home. Théoneste was also lost, because he liked the verandas frequented by high-society types at Heaven. Jean, the public prosecutor, was transferred, and Doctor Georges passed away, taking his jokes and medical genius with him. Moved by the mysteries of migration, the friends then set out again to empty fresh bottles at another boutique at the end of the road.

They landed at Mama Nema's. The proprietor, another handsome and kindhearted woman, welcomed them with loving arms, and they picked up where they left off. Night has fallen on the crowd of people climbing up the hillside. They disperse into courtyards, some of which are lit solely by a single brazier for the evening meal. Fires glow red at the market below as vendors cut prices on the last of the vegetables. Along the thickets, the shadows of cows driven by the silhouettes of cowherds stealthily return from grazing in the bush, a practice now banned by Rwanda's land reforms. Mama Nema hauls out cases of beer with the help of her son. When there aren't enough, the boy hustles down the hill on his bike for more. The friends comment on the latest of the day's news.

Tonight, Emmanuel is describing his most recent agricultural

experiments. Since he left his position with the district administration, he and John and other friends have embarked on a ven-
ture about which they are particularly enthusiastic: the restoration
and renovation of former plantations—with olive and coffee trees
and intensive pig farming. Then someone asks Emmanuel about
the marriage whose negotiations he has agreed to undertake. As a
scrupulous negotiator, and no less as a storyteller, he is very
much in demand. The group discusses the families of the future
bride and groom. Chicago turns up, teary-eyed, unsteady, with a
beaming smile, after a hard day's work in Kigali. Benoît arrives
from his cowshed.

Innocent has suddenly picked a fight with a bewildered
stranger. He presses his case with an orator's rhetoric and a lawyer's
gesticulations. The audience is enjoying itself, listening for the
one insight or remark in Innocent's rhetorical flights they know
will be worth remembering. He indulges in throes of anguish,
never retreats before a provocation, and couldn't care less about
making people uncomfortable. Then, suddenly, he sits back down,
chuckles as he rubs his head, and launches into a funny story about
a Tutsi cow. Everyone laughs. Politics, of the kind that might prove
unpleasant, are never mentioned, except, that is, when someone
has exceeded the limit of inebriation—in which case all impropri-
eties are forgiven.

They talk about their projects. They laugh about everything
and make fun of one another. They discuss the genocide night after
night. If a wave of sadness overtakes them, they wait for it to pass,
bottle of beer in hand. Just now, Concessa, Gonzalve's wife, enters
discreetly. She whispers a knowing word in Mama Nema's ear, then
taps her husband, who is asleep in a chair, and takes him by the arm
to lead him back home. On other nights, Dominique's or Chicago's
wife will do the same.

In the darkness, the din from the hair salons disappears all at once. The crickets burst into a terrific evening racket. The moon outlines the black ridges of mountains to the west. The night firmament gradually appears above our heads, and the shooting stars streak with joy across the sky.

INNOCENT RWILILIZA

TUTSI TEACHER

Father of Ange and Immaculée

I TEACH POLITICAL HISTORY AT THE SECONDARY school. At the start of each academic year, the first question that any new student asks reveals their ethnicity. Hutu and Tutsi youngsters pose different questions about history—their concerns are completely unalike. Students aren't anxious in the same way; they don't use the same words. Young Hutus would just as well not talk about it if they could.

Government directives have banned the words "Hutu" and "Tutsi" from the Rwandan language. Every mention of ethnicity has vanished from official forms; civics has erased ethnic distinctions. Nevertheless, school curricula place a great deal of importance on the history of the Tutsi genocide—they use the term "Tutsi genocide"—and explain that one ethnicity attempted to exterminate the other. From there, even an infant can figure out which ethnicity raised the machete. Because children know from an early age the ethnicity they belong to by listening to their parents, they very quickly place their family within that history. We can't continue to lie to students as we once did about something that has so disturbed their childhoods. When we do, children risk tuning everything out, even lessons on the different types of mammals or the course of a river.

You've already heard as much: the children of survivors reproach themselves nothing. Unlike many survivor parents, they feel blameless. They claim that nothing frightens them, they say they are untroubled. They don't find it awkward to converse with those of their family who remain. But there are truths that they disguise, truths that they still can't bring to light. They hide a terrible desire for vengeance. They hold it deep down inside along with the hate they feel for their families' murderers and the rage they feel when poverty afflicts them. They keep these feelings from their parents in order not to worry them or to avoid a scolding. They turn away, even from the eyes of their closest friends, for fear of reproof. They obey the policy of reconciliation without a word, without betraying their innermost thoughts.

THIS WAS A big thing when I taught at Nelson Mandela Middle School in Kanzenze in the late 1990s. Hutu students didn't dare walk through the classroom door because they were afraid of being harassed by their survivor classmates. We also saw survivor students trembling with fear because someone had left an anonymous note threatening to cut them down like their families had been. Their classmates were taking revenge for their papas' imprisonment. We teachers had to keep a close eye. Children screamed or sulked. We had some who would disappear for three weeks, then suddenly return without a word. Some students refused to listen to the school adviser or psychologist if he belonged to the other ethnicity. Many of them couldn't even think anymore because of the farming they did to feed their brothers and sisters or because of carrying supplies to Rilima. Others roamed around in search of cannabis or alcohol.

In the days after the genocide, no reasonable person could imagine that he wouldn't be killed within the next ten years. The future was cut short. Twenty years have passed, and the neighbors of the two camps have grown accustomed to the idea of dying of old age or disease. They think twice about drowning their defeatism in drink. They have given up spending the night with any old acquaintance for fear of being alone or for something extra to eat. They are less devoted to their own despair. Hope for an ordinary life has returned, although no one understands the reason why. Their children are calmer because of it. They put the enmity they grew up with behind them, and they turn the pages of their schoolbooks in class. They sing about reconciliation. But they don't forget any of the things they keep bottled up. Just like all the others, my own children keep quiet. But I know what is going on.

Survivor children conceal their fear as well. Jean-Damascène and certain other Hutu children blame the high cost of *minervals*. Quite often, though, they held the small sum they needed but backed away from school for fear of their schoolmates' mean intentions. Sandra says that she isn't afraid of the machetes anymore, that she walks through whatever neighborhood she likes. Then she adds that the looks of former prisoners frighten her. When survivor children keep repeating that nothing scares them anymore, isn't it just a way of burying their fear?

What surprises me is that the children of the killers admit that their fathers' crimes have made a mess of their lives—for example, Fabiola and Jean-Damascène—even if they are quick to point out that they don't know exactly what their fathers did. They know, of course. Fabiola saw the long column of killers coming back from Rilima after the presidential pardon in 2003, without her papa and the other category-one criminals. But to say that her papa was in the front line of those plying the machete would mean accusing him of a crime. Maybe in a group of rowdy kids, one or another might have the nerve to call her father an imbecile. In front of an adult, never. In the last twenty years in the Bugesera, it's unheard of. The wrongdoers' children feel apprehensive everywhere. They dread putting their fathers in danger. Look at Fulgence: he was given a twelve-year sentence, then released after seven. He returns to his parcel for seven years as if nothing had happened. He sings the glories of forgiveness everywhere he is asked to speak; he returns to the prosperity of his drink business. Then one Sunday evening they take him back to prison for life. It strikes too much fear in a child.

Some children do feel humiliated by what they know of their parents. They are especially bothered by the defeat. We mustn't forget: their parents just barely lost the battle for extermination, they gave up the leadership of the country they had held in their hands for more than thirty years. They left their possessions behind and sometimes coveted positions in the civil service when they fled. Captivity exhausted their strength. The children saw their parents scurrying back to their fields, humiliated, their shoulders stooped when they spoke to the authorities. Some felt resentment toward those who humbled and bent their parents in this way. In the children's eyes, the punishment, more than justice, caused their misfortune. That's why they have redoubled their efforts to regain their former prosperity. From the moment the sun comes up, they are out tilling the soil, sowing and harvesting, and carefully counting their sacks of crops hidden from prying eyes.

Young Hutus are also deceiving themselves when they say they would freely accept a Tutsi girlfriend or boyfriend. Can I see into their hearts? No, how could I? That said, how many mixed marriages have we seen on Saturdays in Nyamata? Not a single one, to my knowledge. In Kigali, things are different; it's more chaotic. On the hills, the families know each other. They never turn their eyes from the stakes planted around their plots. They never forget inheritances.

AS FOR ME, growing up in the 1960s, I was haunted by the thought that my papa might be taken away or killed. It weighed on us constantly, because not a year went by without killings in the area. I experienced an unhappier childhood than my children. We were driven out of Ruhengeri and endured severe poverty in an adobe hut. We cleared a nearby piece of land to feed ourselves on sweet potatoes and beans. We wanted for everything but fear. We walked five kilometers to fetch water, five kilometers to go to school, and every encounter gave us a fright. My parents were always on the alert—they never smiled for more than a brief moment. If the neighbors shared *urwagwa* with us, it was very nearly a secret. The only recreation without risk: Sunday mass and my mama's bedtime nursery rhymes. Despite all this, good fortune propelled me to the doors of the École normale supérieure. On the day of the entrance exams, I was worried that ethnic quotas would sabotage the results. We faced off, our heads bent over our tests in mutual suspicion. This daily anxiety never let up enough to allow happiness into my childhood.

Nowadays, the children say that they don't consider themselves in danger. But children listen to their parents with keen ears. How could they fail to notice the fears burning in our memories?

SACKS OF BEANS AT ALPHONSE AND CONSOLÉE'S PLACE

IN THE PAST, A SMALL ROAD LED FROM THE MAIN route to Alphonse Hitiyaremye and Consolée Murekatete's place, but the road's collapse has made it impassable even on foot. We now have to make the trip by way of Kibungo instead, turning off at the entrance to Nyarunazi. No matter: Nyarunazi is worth the detour, having surpassed Kibungo as the new center of business on the hill. In the market at night, women bargain in whispers in the glow of kerosene lamps. Early in the morning and throughout the day, one hears a string of choirs' hymns under the lofty acacia trees, situated far from the temptations of the street. A long, colonnaded building has sprung up at the same time as the handsome homes of Nyamata's nouveaux riches. A "saloon" displays its brand-new sign beside modest *urwagwa* bars. The weather grows hot in the middle of the afternoon and sweltering at dusk. Women attend to their sewing machines, chitchat at the market, or sing with their loving eyes fixed on the strutting preachers. Men drink in the street. Gone is the day, not so long ago, when one saw Tutsi cabarets at one end and Hutu at the other. After a day in the fields, people now drink freely with whoever passes the *chalumeau* along.

Eustache staggers down the street as he makes his way to greet me. A regular at the cabarets at this time of day, he offers me a very warm welcome. He deserves a Primus. Eustache is a friend from my first days in Rwanda, when he oversaw Nyamata's public telephone. Indeed, he still asks me for news about the Depardon family, whose conversations he listened to when Raymond Depardon, the photographer whose work appears in *Life Laid Bare*, joined me in Nyamata, just as he overheard every other call before the advent of cell phones. This former post office manager is one of the rare Hutus alive whose conduct during the killings arouses no suspicion—many of the others were murdered. Among the exceptions were two veterinarians as well as the three Pentecostal farmhands who chose to join the Tutsis in the Kayumba forest rather than take up the machete. Strangely, they disappeared afterward, probably for Ruhengeri. Currently retired, Eustache farms his parcel every morning except on Sundays and drinks every day in the afternoon. He can sometimes be found, out of breath, his mind in a whirl of violent anger, in pursuit of a black goat—always the same goat, according to him—which has supposedly eloped with one of his new does. He generally returns home late at night on his splendid bicycle, which no doubt knows its way back to Nyamata, where his wife, who certainly knows her husband, is waiting up for him.

JUST OUTSIDE NYARUNAZI, after a stretch of scrubland, the road runs along a hillside beside a valley of lush banana groves sheltered from the sun by the steep topography. Such a landscape is difficult to imagine in the Bugesera. The trees are pruned, sometimes propped up under the weight of bananas. The palms appear a lustrous green; the ocher soil seems washed clean. We run into Pio and Josiane on their bicycles. The mileage covered by this pair of lovers is incredible. Yesterday, we passed them on the road to Ntarama. They were visiting an aunt to discuss the sale of their land prior to their move to the Mutara region. Two days earlier, we spotted them at the market, and shortly before that, at the clinic. Josiane, upset with me for previously revealing certain episodes from their love affair, suggests we make peace. Before they leave, she even tries half-jokingly to negotiate royalties on certain unknown chapters of their story, probably thinking of the cost of their impending departure for the Mutara.

The route regains the blinding sun in Nyamabuye. Consolée, dripping wet and joyful in the middle of her courtyard, breaks off from threshing bean plants to open her home to us. Whatever the time of year, sacks of seeds and grain clutter her living room like a warehouse. She and her husband, Alphonse, labor to make up for lost time. Alphonse wasn't able to return to his former business, but he has proved remarkably successful in developing their two plots of land. They are serious farmers. They have started to rear crossbred cows. They are experimenting with coffee and fruit trees. Their banana groves are radiant, their fields furrowed as straight as arrows. Thanks to their relentlessness, Alphonse and Consolée are less affected by the vicissitudes of the weather than other farmers are. While they were too late to save Jean-Pierre's education, their eldest boy is pursuing his studies at the National University, their oldest girl has found a place in a sewing shop on Nyamata's main street, and their little ones work hard at school.

In Rilima, at the time of my book *Machete Season*, Alphonse was the least reluctant of his gang to pay genuine attention to the answers he gave. During his imprisonment, Consolée was the only prisoner's wife who dared to break the Hutu code of silence, who agreed to describe what life was like for the wives during the killings. It was she who told me one day: "Myself, I was afraid. I was obsessed by a divine malediction. I could plainly see that those unnatural killings would bring about a punishment from heaven, that all the blood was going to bring down damnation. I knew that God might step in at any moment like in the Bible. I thought about Egypt, Gomorrah, and the like."

Today, Alphonse works himself body and soul as part of two farming cooperatives—one of sugarcane growers, the other of farmers of foodstuffs—for which he organizes the mutual-aid raffles. Consolée is active in a number of community associations. During the *gaçaça* trials, she was named an *inyangamugayo*, a person of integrity, and in that capacity presided over her sector's jury and pushed stubbornly to allow survivors and killers the opportunity to speak.

Alphonse, alerted by the car engine and dripping with sweat, doesn't take long to join us. We exchange news about our common acquaintances. Adalbert Munzigura, who disappeared for several years in a seedy part of Kigali, has resurfaced, and not in any old way—he has finally gotten married. They see him from time to time en route to his sister's place. After three years of marriage, Pancrace Hakizamungili's third child was born. He is jubilant, although he recently mourned the death of his mother. In the evenings, he devotes himself to community volunteering, especially door-to-door work for the national census. Alphonse and Consolée refrain from sharing their thoughts about Fulgence's situation. Alphonse claims to know nothing about the latter's involvement in Ernestine's murder. He hasn't gone to visit him or Joseph-Désiré in Rilima, but he receives news from Fulgence's wife, Jacqueline, whom they run into most often in Nyarunazi. Jean-Baptiste Murangira has resigned himself to struggling along in farming, which leaves him little more than the skin on his bones.

He would never have accepted such a life were his Tutsi wife, Spéciose, not setting the example in the fields. Consolée and Alphonse can't help making fun of him. They laugh when I recount the afternoon of endless argument and Primus beers with Ignace and Jeanne after Ignace's return from the reeducation camp.

Then we speak about the children.

ALPHONSE HITIYAREMYE AND CONSOLÉE MUREKATETE

HUTU FARMERS

Parents of Jean-Pierre

ALPHONSE: WHEN I WAS THREE, A MYSTERIOUS ILLNESS killed my father; when I was ten, a fever carried off my mother. A relative gave me shelter in exchange for odd jobs. In my fourteenth year, the hoe held out its handle for me to find food. I didn't finish primary school. That's a drawback that persists to this day. A prosperous farmer adopted me as his son for my strength in the field. He gave me my chance in farming. I raised crops, I bought land, and I was happily wed to Consolée.

Before the genocide, we were somewhat well-to-do. We farmed two fertile parcels near the water. The banana plantation gave in abundance. It wasn't every Hutu who owned cows like mine. The genocide drove us back into poverty. I spent seven years in Rilima. Consolée didn't give up farming. She put her admirable energy into the harvests and the schoolwork for the children's education. Porridge for meals, gathering wood, cleaning—it was difficult, but it wasn't miserable. Which is why I say now, today, that if the children were knocked off course because of me, they still experienced a childhood with less suffering than mine.

CONSOLÉE: When we returned from Congo, everything set the children trembling. They were always on the alert. They stopped listening to instructions, and their minds deserted their lessons. When they were harassed with vengeful taunts on the way to school, they obviously asked me why. They reasoned as little ones do; they had lived in exile in the camps. It was risky explaining the actual causes to them. They might become discouraged at school or stand up to the survivor children to fight. So I sidestepped. I answered, "Be brave. The attacks won't last. It's just a bunch of derelict kids." They heard the gossip on the hill, they learned the lessons about the genocide at school, and they seemed afraid. They grew bolder. They insisted on knowing why their papa remained in prison. They weren't worried about the machetes or the reasons for the battles. The killings didn't kindle their curiosity. They wanted to know what their papa had done wrong, his character, when he would be released. First I tried to protect them. I told them, "Be careful. The survivors have suffered to their very bones. They might want to do us harm. Thoughts of vengeance inflame them. Watch that you behave humbly." Then I explained how we had been contaminated by the war. I explained the killings, the defeat, and our escape to Congo. Back then, we spoke of war. Over the years, we had gotten used to the word "war," *intambara*, or "killing," *ubwicanyi*. Basically, we didn't really understand what the word "genocide" meant. We didn't want to risk understanding. In our family, the children brought the word home from school.

ALPHONSE: One day, my eldest boy came to visit me. I handed him a piece of paper for my wife. In the message, I wrote, "I confess. It's no use denying anymore." Consolée wasn't ignorant of my misdeeds. How could she be? In the morning, she saw me leave with the expeditions, in the front line ahead of my colleagues. And at night, I came home with my clothes stinking of blood and mud. She understood what I had confessed. She could speak to the children with honest words. Basically, the explanations the mamas gave their children depended on the conduct of the prisoners: If they denied all involvement in the killings, the mamas withheld every truth from their children. If they confessed a little to the judges, the mamas told the children a little—in other words, what the papas had agreed upon with the authorities. In our family, it was a big thing, thanks to Consolée.

CONSOLÉE: It's different for the Tutsis. The people who experienced the machetes suffer from sadness, and from anger, too. They have no trouble giving details to back up their explanations. The parents speak forcefully of their sorrows to their children. Their memories don't distort things much. The more you suffer injustice in life, the more you ask yourself the right questions, and the more you dig around for answers.

For the wrongdoers, the release from prison gives you the courage to speak. In Rilima, waiting in line with the other wives, we didn't talk about our children. Each guilty family zigzagged in its own way. Today still, many wrongdoers fine-tune the lies about their time in Congo; they grumble, their fingers pointed at the survivors. Their children sulk. The children, like their parents, beat around the bush, claim they don't know anything because there is nothing to know. But the truth lurks about. They bump against it because they listen to their classmates. They hear the gossip. During the *gaçaças*, so many children crawled through the grass like little bandits trying to slip their ears in among the public.

ALPHONSE: When I left, I was mended. Today, I help my wife with the children's education, since it is above all their mama they listen to. I tell them bit by bit, at night after the meal or in the fields. No child has ever called me bad. But they feel blameworthy for what they hear. They get hung up and keep to the side if they come across young people their age. It upsets them deep down inside. It obviously troubles me to leave them that to inherit. Wouldn't someone who doesn't feel this way be dangerous?

CONSOLÉE: Do children in other families get angry with their parents? Who knows. I have seen some who ask forgiveness in their parents' place. In our family, anyway, the children carry the burden of the genocide. The children learn about brutality from a young age. They hear stories of machetes drenched in blood. Gossip eats away at them, and poverty pens them in. They endure the work in the fields. We adults have ruined their innocence. Basically, they were denied a happy childhood. Young people from both ethnicities are connected in this way. I mean, the lack of innocence connects them.

We combined our strength to encourage them. Our children don't smoke cannabis. When they go to the market to sell crops, they buy something for the family. They don't waste; they put the money in their pocket. They don't drink much Primus. You don't see them rebelling. They sit with their family at church. You see them good-natured. They still seem timid, though. We can see they have been affected. They have been hindered at school. The best grades have eluded them. Jean-Pierre, for example, studied too hastily. He sacrificed the end-of-year prizes and the compliments they give the best students. Over time, we have learned to live with that. That's how I raise them.

SYLVIE'S TEMPLE

THE TEMPLE OF ZION IS HOUSED UNDER A SHED roof propped between tall acacias. On this crude frame fabrics hang, providing decoration but doing little to insulate the faithful from the scorching heat or the sudden showers that pour down during the rainy season. The structure also fails to shield the congregants from the powerful PA system that blares the pastors' sermons at top volume. This explains why, after several locations in town, the temple was obliged to move beyond the local cabaret courtyards to the edge of the bush.

Pastors founded the Zion Temple Celebration Center in Kigali in 1999, establishing themselves at the same time as a vast number of other congregations in what had become the troubled territory of the Catholic Church. Five years after the genocide, the temple's theology of spiritual awakening and miracles reassured believers whose faith had been shaken with doubt. Even without understanding a word of Kinyarwanda, visitors can't help being impressed by the show the feverish preachers put on and, in particular, by the furious beauty of the congregation's spirituals.

On this Sunday, at the entrance to the makeshift church, a woman wearing a magnificent red priestess's dress welcomes her flock. The woman is Sylvie. She encourages a newcomer, hugs a lady friend, caresses a child, and lavishes her well-wishes on the new arrivals, never once losing the joyful good cheer I observed in her the very first day we met. A wonder to behold is the procession of families in their Sunday best, taking their places on the rustic benches as the electric organ fills the air. Exceedingly beautiful ladies linger near the altar, their loving eyes riveted on the preachers who warm themselves up with syncopated hallelujahs, as sure of their charisma as of their faith. The chorus begins its breathtaking hymns. The synthesizers are now going full bore. It's a big day for Sylvie, the deaconess, who climbs on stage.

IN A WORLD without machetes, Sylvie Umubyeyi's fate would have followed the favor of her youth: her immense family in Butare, her vocation, her energy and passion, her kindness, her colorful sense of humor. But her family was wiped out near the National University campus in Butare, and humiliation awaited her in exile in Bujumbura. In Nyamata, in the harsh Bugesera where she chose to resume her life as a social worker, she discovered the devastation of the human soul. Later, the mistake of a humanitarian organization forced her into exile in Tanzania. When she returned, she faced family turmoil, not to mention health problems, which would have crushed others in the same situation. Because of this, her presence amid the mystic pandemonium of the Temple of Zion is hardly surprising. Judging by her perpetually playful smile, there isn't much to worry about.

It was in a bar in Kigali that a journalist first told me her story. Four years after the genocide in a marshy area deep in the Bugesera hills, he had met a social worker crisscrossing the bush in her van on the lookout for stray children. The small town was Nyamata, which I reached at the end of a rocky path the next day. The story was true. The social worker's name was Sylvie Umubyeyi. Accompanying her into the bush opened up an initial path for me to follow into the heart of my book *Life Laid Bare*.

We got into her Toyota. At the top of the hill, we continued the rest of the way on foot until we reached a small adobe house within a well-tended banana plantation. Jeannette and Chantal lived there, two orphans surrounded by a pack of little kids rescued after years of brutal existence in the bush, where they had taken refuge from the machetes. We spent the afternoon talking with Jeannette. Sylvie also spoke about her work, which, according to her, she made up as she went along.

As Sylvie explained to me at the time: "To weave a bond with a child battered about by the genocide, the first thing you have to do is encourage him to open up a little bit and to unload some of his thoughts—that's where the knots of his trouble come through. Me, I follow a simple strategy. I approach the child, I keep silent for a brief moment, then I say to him: 'Just like you, I am a survivor. Just like you, I saw them do all they could to end my life. Just like you, I know that my entire family is dead. I saw the *interahamwe* only a few feet in front of me stabbing people with their spears. The two of us are going to have to live with these truths from now on' . . . Sharing the genocide in words with someone who lived through it is different from sharing it with someone who learned about it somewhere else. After a genocide, a wound remains buried deep in the survivor's spirit, a wound that can never be brought into the full light of day. We survivors, we may not know the exact nature of this hidden wound, but at least we know that it exists . . . Those who escaped the machetes will never be free of their experiences, but they can find the way back to life because they can speak the truth. They fear many dangers but not the danger of lies. The children who survived the Nyamwiza marshes have peered into the darkest of evil, but only for a short time. If you take hold of them and gently guide them along, things come more easily . . . For Hutu children who went to Congo, the burden remains, because they haven't faced the past directly. Silence paralyzes them with fear. Time is against them. Some of their parents are in prison, but if you ask them if they know the reason, they dodge your questions . . . They are afraid of being mistreated . . . As the years pass, they feel more and more guilty for their parents' bad actions. Nothing changes from visit to visit. You notice that their anxieties are constantly chasing away other thoughts. You do your best to encourage them to speak, but they won't be able to regain their footing in life if they never say a word about the turmoil within them. So you have to be very gentle and patient with them, trusting to time the birth of a new friendship . . .

"Children often fall into a deep distress or panic, especially when they sleep. They reproduce in dream what they experienced in life. They cry out, they sob, sometimes they take off running into the night or ask to be forgiven."

WE MEET UP after mass at the Savana cabaret. Sylvie seems happy with her performance as deaconess. She laughs at having imposed it on me. She is the first to mention the good memories from fifteen years ago, when we met on a sweltering afternoon. Nothing moved on the main street, crushed by heat and sadness, except for the rare pedestrians in search of a bottle and some herdsmen urging along their scraggy cows. The humanitarian organization where she worked had its offices in the former house of a town notable. Sylvie had come out into the yard. Her flowery dress accentuated her pregnancy. She held a notebook and a pen in her hand. She was beaming. Her eyes sparkled with mischief, and her smile intrigued me. Something was making her laugh, but what was it? Was it the sight of a bewildered journalist amid the desolation of this little town?

SYLVIE UMUBYEYI

TUTSI SOCIAL WORKER

YOU REMEMBER THE FIRST TIME WE MET? IT WAS in 1997 in the yard outside the World Vision offices. I was working with the stray children of the genocide at the time. They were turning up everywhere. Some lived in families that weren't their own; others no longer had families because they had seen their parents die. There were children scattered in the bush and forest, and we went looking for them with the van. The work interested me because I was holding as close as I could to the genocide. I managed to do something worthwhile. I united families of children with adolescent heads of family to care for them. They've grown up and returned to the school bench. They've led good lives, first as children, then as adolescents. Those that have gotten married are raising their own children now. A small number have gone to university, and the others have picked up a trade.

You saw Jeannette yesterday? How's she doing these days? Is she still sewing in the market? I know she married a bike-taxi driver named Sylvestre. Did they go through with their adventure in the Mutara? . . . Oh dear, them, too? And they lasted just two dreadful years? They're up to three children, I've been told. You know, when I run into them or hear about them, I can see that life has slipped back into their everyday experiences. I'm proud of that.

Why was I willing to help you in your work? Because that's my job as a social worker. A French journalist all alone on Nyamata's main street, four years after the killings—it seemed like either someone in dire need of assistance or someone inexplicably trying to rile people up. You might have lost your way, too, without anyone to stand beside you. The folks around here talked—so many rumors mixed with mean words. As usual, people carried on for as long as they remained suspicious. Things weren't going to be easy. People said, "That Tutsi woman walking around with a Frenchman—is she really Tutsi?" There were some who tattled, who called my husband: "She just passed down the main street with the *muzungu*. They're sharing a bottle at the parish. We saw them in her truck over in Ntarama . . ."

I had to work inside my own head, I mean, without listening, and speaking as little as possible. It wasn't so risky, though. I was coming from Butare myself, so I seemed a foreigner, too. I had the reputation of folks from Butare and didn't have the bullheaded mentality of people from the Bugesera. I thought, all right, let's give it a try. I listened; your words weren't intended to hurt people. You didn't set traps. You hesitated. A man who hesitates, you can put him right. You showed yourself steady. I realized that you wouldn't be stingy with your time, that you would hear them out. In those days, survivors were so afraid that no one would listen to their sometimes chaotic words. It was painful not to be really heard. They lost the courage; they grew used to staying silent. Like me, you tried to get closer to the genocide.

I can't say that it helped me. It surprised me a bit. Could I imagine a book about the Nyamata survivors at a time when fear ate away at me, when those around me felt blameworthy, when no one knew what path to take to live again? No, I thought the work might be a good thing. Basically, though, our jobs intersect: sitting on a bench at people's sides, thinking about the questions to ask, listening to the words at work behind the stories, without neglecting the silences or the past, and following them wherever they lead.

MYSELF, HOWEVER, I didn't want to sit by my children's side to tell them the story of the genocide. That surprises you? It doesn't surprise me. And yet that's how it was. Before my parents' funeral, it may still have been possible, while I was still very upset. In the years that followed the machetes, I did everything I could to find out where and how my papa and mama had been cut in Butare. The question preyed on my mind. It was like an obsession. I was traumatized, so to speak, although I hid it from people's eyes. Then I received the news about the massacre of my family. I got the details and I wept. I went to Butare with my children and my sister Claudine to arrange the funeral service. We appealed to God. A great relief suddenly took hold of my heart. The trembling and deathly visions went away.

I finally calmed down. Gone were the evenings spent remembering the worst moments of suffering, of mourning the dead, of piling up rumors instead of facts. My heart was unburdened, as I told you, of anguish if not of fear. My confidence in others—I see that it is more or less ruined for good, but I have confidence in myself and in those I love. There was a time I had lost everything, when I felt I always needed to speak about the extermination, the loss, and the shame. You wrote those words. Courage returned, followed by my taste for life. I don't want to be disappointed by existence anymore. So why would I let it disappoint my children? The scenes of the genocide are no longer so present that I feel compelled to tell my children about them. I don't have the time. Why offer them sorrow? No, no, I don't hide anything, but I don't want to force on them the evil that has made me suffer.

Even if life has stopped for some people, it continues for the children. That's something I learned from my parents. As I told you, we lived in a big, very loving family of two hundred people in Butare. As early as 1959, my parents were driven out, then again in the 1960s. My grandparents were killed, the cows eaten, the houses burned. That was the saga of the Tutsis. When my mama started telling us about their youth, explaining to us how badly the wicked Hutus had mistreated them, my papa interrupted her: "No, we mustn't speak about it to the children. This evil has harmed us, but they must be protected. It might poison them."

My parents pampered me in childhood. They surrounded me with love for life. Maybe I have tried to imitate them. I thought, the machetes killed my parents, not the strength they gave me. What the ears of my children must hear, they will hear elsewhere. As for myself, I must raise them as I was raised. I want life to stretch out far in front of them, without the blood. When a person has been the cause of bloody misdeeds against your family, and that person constantly comes up in adult conversations, children listen; they wonder why that terrible person is still living on their hill. The question infects their childhood with a sense of injustice, and they grow up with resentment. It's a big thing to spoil their development in this way.

But I don't hide anything from my children. I don't evade their questions. In April, when they watch the shows on television, when they talk about them, I provide the explanations they ask for. Do they have questions? Not very many. Aurore was five years old at the time of the genocide, Gabin three, and I was pregnant with the third. All three have memories of the killings or of the hardship that came afterward: the exile in Bujumbura, the return to Nyamata, the poverty. They haven't ever asked me a single question. No, not ever. Why, I don't know. A photograph of my mama is sitting in the living room. Not once have they asked me details about her. There she is and they say nothing. Only the youngest ones, Carmen and Annelyse, who were born much later, have asked me questions: "Why don't you have any parents?" I tell them about how my family was killed. "You ran away to Burundi, why?" I tell them how we escaped with our lives on the road to Bujumbura. They aren't looking for details about the machetes or the Hutus.

My children aren't ones to poke around in family history. Maybe they don't want to make me sad. In any case, they see that, unlike before, I no longer get up from bed with grim visions in my eyes. With their childhood lucidity, they probably steer clear of the words that might hurt me. It's a bit unclear. I imagine that the history doesn't interest them, as simple as that. They think that it's a disagreement among adults, and it can only cause them trouble. Maybe they sidestep because of their papa.

My husband is very traumatized. He is a highly regarded teacher: his expertise is valued as far away as South Africa. The genocide devastated him. He hates bringing it up. If he speaks of it, he feels emotions he can do nothing to control. Wickedness rises before his eyes. His words come rushing out, he threatens all the Hutus, and his lips stir up the anger that his heart only whispers. His movements are unpredictable. He becomes someone else, thrashing about in the throes of a psychological disorder. During the commemorations, he drinks and smokes. As soon as he gets home, we have to be quiet. He sits down lifeless in a corner of the house. He no longer has time for the children. He stops speaking. The children stay away from him. I don't know if they are frightened of him, if they worry for him. We don't discuss it. It's a burden. We steer clear. The genocide pushes us to accept what we thought would be impossible to accept. We draw from a mysterious force to keep going.

THIS REFUSAL TO bring up the genocide happened without my thinking about it. No, you're mistaken—religion didn't enter into it. I have always prayed with the same sincerity. Nowadays, it's with the Pentecostals. I discovered the Temple of Zion during my time in Tanzania because their parish was located next door. When I came back to Nyamata, I stuck with them. Before that, I belonged to the Catholic Church—nothing bad to say about it. I didn't leave over theological differences or because of the pastors. Here's the reason: In a Catholic mass, you sometimes find yourself elsewhere—you return to other thoughts, often sad ones. You drift off into grim memories. Fervor doesn't sweep you along the way it does with the Pentecostals. The music and the sermons carry you away. We sing, we listen. Rejoicing helps us commune with God.

The Pentecostal Church has changed my behavior. An example? I used to drink beer. I would drink after service. I could spend much too much time drinking with acquaintances in secluded places. I wouldn't enter a cabaret with just anyone; with two or three friends, then I had the courage. Before the genocide, I wouldn't even have had a sip. That came later. Despair closed in around me, and minor marriage problems wore me down, as they do so many others. I looked for places to hide. Here in Rwanda, a man who drinks makes a lot of friends. A woman, too. It's not a happy thing, not even pleasant; it's comforting. You didn't notice? Because I know how to control myself, like all Rwandan women. So you start habits that aren't good. You distract yourself with things that aren't very respectable. No examples!

Nowadays, I do both. I drink a little bit of beer, only when I feel like it, and I pray and sing as much as I like, whenever I like.

Religion supports me in raising the children. It helps me to hold them close. I didn't convince them to believe. I brought them along several Sundays, and just like that, they were full of enthusiasm. They sing in the choir, they devote their time to the associations. They're happy at the church. You heard him, my son playing electric organ on Sunday. Their vacations are taken up with church activities. That's how they build their confidence despite their worries.

It's not only at church. My children are filled with enthusiasm for many different educational and recreational activities at school. They go to youth clubs, music, computers, and movies—they are very open-minded. No arguments or rude remarks when it comes to chores at home. It was through their activities at school that they got their education about the genocide, the same as their education about AIDS prevention or drugs. They assemble to talk, they visit the memorials, they watch the documentaries. They receive an education about the genocide outside of the family.

The children who have seen the worst, like my three eldest, will never get over it. But I think they are at ease; I don't notice any fear in them, anyway. Life doesn't trouble them. They don't close their hearts. In my work, I have been enormously involved with children traumatized by the genocide. You saw me searching for them in the bush. I loved this work deeply. Oftentimes, a child's trauma comes to him from having a keener and more precocious intelligence than his peers do. The more intelligent he is, the more it will make him suffer.

CLAUDINE'S *MUDUGUDU*

WHAT STAR LED ME UP SUCH A STEEP, GULLY-FILLED
path? I had no idea that it would take me past Berthe's house
and then on to Claudine's at the top of the hill. A lucky star, that
much is for sure, because it was by purest good fortune that I made
the acquaintance of Berthe Mwanankabandi and Claudine Kayitesi in that remote setting up there in the bush. They were twenty
years old; a childhood friendship united them. The machetes had
killed their families. Since then, they had taught themselves how
to farm their plots. A pack of children crowded their courtyards:
orphans from around the area whom a humanitarian organization
had placed in their care. Berthe had also given birth to two babies
"born on the sly." Claudine raised her little five-year-old daughter,
born in Congo during her abduction.

It was always a pleasure to chat with them during my stays.
In the beginning, however, although they never appeared hostile,
they took no interest in what might become of their words. They
indulged in conversation because they couldn't imagine the writing of a book and still less the intention behind it. Their curiosity
awoke little by little, each in its own way. Always hospitable, they
became warmhearted; diligent in the beginning, they strove to be

more detailed in their accounts. The impulsive and more distrustful Berthe often responded brusquely. Claudine seemed more fatalistic, ironic, with her occasionally caustic remarks, even if she was no less desperate than Berthe. They sought a way to get more involved. They began to think about what the questions and answers taught them about themselves.

One afternoon, Berthe came to tell me: "Sometimes sleep draws me back into the marshes. I see all those people again, their blood-soaked bodies stretched out in the sludge. I see my parents in dreams, my little sisters and acquaintances. I see the living, who resemble the dead. Everything seems normal and calm. It's good. I'm with those who sleep as gently as the dead. When I wake up, a terrible anguish, or sorrow, is there to greet me, as if I had visited the house of the dead."

Fate separated the two women. Berthe moved into a house with her sister in Ntarama's *mudugudu* at the bottom of the road. One evening, she said: "Deep down, I succumb to a kind of hatred, a fear. Having a husband, living happily as a family—I just don't see it . . . For an orphan survivor, choosing the right husband is a torment. If he has no problems and doesn't understand you, it's no good; if he understands you but has too many problems himself, it's no better . . . I have suffered through too much to risk living with a husband who can't console me when I'm inconsolable. I prefer the anxieties of a woman alone, and giving birth on the sly, obviously, because no woman can give that up."

She is restless, undertakes various projects, which she abandons just as quickly. When the drought-hardened earth wears her down, she drops her tools and takes the bus for Kigali to look for odd jobs as a nurse's aide or salesperson.

Claudine moved farther, three kilometers away, to the Kanzenze *mudugudu*, where she and her new husband, Damascène Bizima, could be nearer to his plot of land. She described their wedding as follows: "It was a grand affair. The choristers opened the ceremony dressed in their decorated *pagnes*. I wore the three traditional dresses and my husband hid his hands in elegant white gloves. The church provided its courtyard and tablecloths. Three vans brought the wedding party, along with Fanta sodas, sorghum wine, and cases of Primus, of course. Our fete lasted three unbelievable days."

Her life follows the rhythms of farming, the routines of her very happy family, and the calendar of church events, with which she stays enthusiastically busy. Not so long ago, however, she made an admission as she talked to me about her life: "Yes, calm has settled in. I have beautiful children, a relatively fertile field, and a nice husband to support me. A few years ago, after the killings, when you met me for the first time, I was a simple girl with stray children all around me. I had nothing except drudgery and bad thoughts. Since then, my husband has turned me into a family lady—I never could have imagined. In the mornings, courage takes me by the hand. Life offers me its smiles and I owe it my thanks for not having abandoned me in the marshes. But still, for me, the chance to become someone has passed. All the questions you ask me—you won't ever hear answers from the real Claudine, because I've pretty much lost my love of myself. I've known the filth of animals, I've seen the ferocity of the hyena and worse still—because animals are never as vile as that. I was called an insect. I was forced by a brutal man. I was taken away, out there, to a place about which nothing can be said. But the worst is still there walking in front of me. My heart will always hold suspicions. It knows all too well that destiny can break its promises."

Claudine was sixteen years old at the time of the killings, just a year younger than her daughter Nadine is now.

CLAUDINE KAYITESI

TUTSI FARMER

Nadine's mother

AS A CHILD, I MADE MY WAY TO SCHOOL IN BARE feet. All the little ones went shoeless to church on Sunday mornings. Today, they wear shoes from an early age, but they walk without parents. Their parents have either been cut or punished, or they conceal their trauma in the dark corner of a courtyard, or they never leave the bottle in the cabaret. Drought sometimes so cracks the earth that it drives women to Kigali alone. You remember Berthe. Whenever the rain runs short, she rushes off to the city, leaving her children in the *mudugudu*. She offers her services in hospital wards or shops in search of a little money for food. Nowadays, it's very lucky for a child to grow up with two actual parents—two people who have their health and freedom.

There are vagrant children wandering about who fear no one. You see them smoking cannabis at the edge of the bush. They sometimes stand in the middle of the road with their cigarette. You make a remark, and they clear off without taking the trouble to run. You can see that nothing frightens them. They have known the wickedness of adults since preschool; they have grown up in their elders' lies. They dare to say whatever they like, and they don't care if they do something wrong. What's the use of distinguishing between good and evil when you have been given evil from the time you were born.

We parents are getting older, and we are weighed down by dreadful memories. We accept the unacceptable, we feign reconciliation. As I told you, we cannot abandon our nature forever. One doesn't live merely on the health benefits of beans. We long to experience something before we die. Fate has camped out at our door and we have gotten used to it. But a lot of children stumble.

I spent my childhood in farming. My parents made a good life from their field. Since they were born Tutsi, they raised handsome cows and goats for the healthy milk. I took care of my brothers and sisters. The courtyard chores were mine, which lessened my mama's burdens. She devoted herself to the hoe. I lent a hand with weeding, and I used a long staff to watch over the animals with other children my age. Our eyes lit up when we saw the herds. Seeing the big-horned animals peacefully eating in the bush stirred our Tutsi pride. The elders intervened in quarrels under the acacia trees. It was good. We could grow up feeling safe. Our papa's and mama's kind help shouldered us up. Those you call "uncles" and "aunts" kept watch.

I received a basic education. My parents took me in hand, and the neighbors, like everywhere in Africa, stepped in to set me right whenever it was needed. The teachers told us what to do. It was carefree, except, of course, for the ethnic fears. Then everything changed; you know why. Now, many children lack a mother's arms in which they can forget their worries. They don't heed advice. They prefer to fend for themselves as they have learned to do alone. If the papa did wrong, if he served a long sentence, it's difficult for a child to understand the meaning of respect. If the parents are dead or traumatized, family authority slips away. Around here, neighbors are powerless, and the priests and teachers simply swallow the government's instructions.

We are living through a fairly chaotic century. Technology kindles greed and encourages one to lie. With the internet, television, and sex videos, nothing is hidden from the children anymore. That's true for all the children in the world. It's riskier, though, for children without parents. They don't know where to find a shoulder to rest their troubled heads. They are never disciplined by an adult's stern voice, and nothing stops them from throwing themselves onto the internet. They go out looking for any kind of entertainment to escape their dark thoughts. They turn to video-game zombies and monsters to keep them company.

IT'S NO SECRET that Nadine is more difficult than I was. She would be even worse if she hadn't chosen the path of the church. I started to talk to her about the genocide when she was thirteen. Until then, she didn't know what had occurred. At least, that's what I thought. She didn't ask a single question. I decided not to upset her. I didn't want to go up to her and say, "There was a genocide. Here's how it happened to our family." I waited patiently for her questions to come. She started to ask me why I didn't have a papa or mama. What had they done to disappear? She had probably already talked about it with her schoolmates.

My answers didn't zigzag. I told her step by step how her grandparents had been killed, like so many others. Why all the Tutsis had been hunted like prey by their Hutu neighbors. We talked about ethnicity, about age-old quarrels and bitter resentments. We chatted about the genocide. From that moment on, she showed herself eager for information when we gathered in the evenings. She became restless during the Week of Mourning.

Then she asked me about my life during the genocide. I told her about the bleak events in the swamps. I didn't shy from my unpleasant life, although I didn't divulge all the secrets. We continue our chats about that past existence if a question comes up.

For example, Nadine wants to know everything about my parents: What their life was like at home, their favorite jokes, if they teased each other for fun, if they knew Rwandan stories and songs. What clothing they wore to church or to ceremonies. What they preferred to eat besides beans. If the ladies also had a taste for the bottle. If they had polished manners, if they were very slender and tall. The kinds of question that restore the family in her imagination. We went to the Rugarama hill to see the old family house. We visited the Ntarama memorial, the place where my parents departed this world.

One day, she asked me about her birth. I was expecting it. She was curious about Congo. She wondered about the landscape. She suddenly wanted to know all the details about her blood papa. I explained to her that she had been conceived by an *interahamwe*. I avoided admitting that I had been forced. Too much sorrow would have been risky. Does she know the whole truth? She has probably heard the gossip from the lips of wicked neighbors. She wouldn't dare tell me, though. We mention this biological papa without going into details. But not often. Sometimes she makes do with sensible questions, other times she asks surprising ones. They bring her down. Sometimes she asks them two or three times, as if she were looking for a new answer. She seems troubled. Certain thoughts disrupt her at school when they are too overwhelming. I support her, I comfort her. Exposing the truth would only add anguish to her sadness. Describing to her how brutally she was conceived—that wouldn't clarify her understanding of things. As the mama, I have no choice but to live with what has been ruined deep within me, but most important, I have to protect her from this misfortune. I simply explain to her how I have grown accustomed to my strange fate.

She's lucky that her faith helps her. No, I wasn't the one who drew her to the church. Nadine would be going to church even if she'd had the gentle life of a young girl brought into the world normally, even if she'd been prancing around among loving grandparents. God guides her. He steadies her when she stumbles on her path. She joins the kindly believers to pray. The songs distract her from sorrow. Faith keeps her from wasting too much time thinking about harmful things. She is sincere.

Modern times push children to be precocious. As I said, at twelve years old they search through things on the internet that we learned about only after marriage. On the hills, it's even more terrible than elsewhere. Young people fled their childhood to protect themselves from the wickedness of adults. They felt terror when they listened to the stories. They trembled hearing the rumors. Fear has abandoned them. They no longer feel in danger—they ply their machetes in the banana groves without giving it a second thought. Yet they have been affected all the same. They're hiding out. Their hearts whisper for revenge for the mistreatment of their parents. It's inevitable in the two ethnicities. But these young people can't express it. Too many disapproving looks force them to keep quiet. They shelter things even from their closest friends. Have I noticed the same in Nadine? No, that's her secret.

It is always possible that she likes a Hutu boy, without mentioning him to me, and that one of these days she is going to bring him home, with his white gloves, to meet me. If he is a good Christian, I will entrust them to the hands of God. And what if the suitor doesn't believe in God? Can you even imagine?

THE FUTURE

NADINE UMUTESI

SEVENTEEN YEARS OLD

Daughter of Claudine Kayitesi, Tutsi survivor

IF ONE DAY MY BLOOD PAPA WERE TO APPEAR before me, I would ask him his name, the work he does, and where he lives. That's it. I wouldn't listen to the rest—I wouldn't care. I am saying the opposite of what I told you the last time because I have had the chance to reflect. I was surprised by your question. Basically, before you asked, I had never imagined it, I had never thought about seeing him for real. I knew that whether or not I met him, no good would come of it either way. I have chosen Damascène as my true papa, even though he didn't give me life. Since my earliest childhood, Damascène has truly taken the other man's place. We live in joyful harmony. Every day he shows me a father's kindness, and he offers me a father's guidance. He's a good worker and very strong. He speaks easily with everyone, he sings with all his might, and he doesn't drink alcohol. During negotiations for my marriage, I know that he'll conceal the shameful circumstances of my birth, that he'll slip on his ceremonial gloves. My parents see eye to eye about me. They waited for the rumors to begin before explaining my birth because they were anxious to protect me. They were afraid that bad thoughts might ruin my childhood.

I was kind of shaken up. When a child lives with such an extraordinary fact, she really feels uneasy growing up. Yes, I ask myself questions that other young people my age don't ask themselves. I live with the risk of a terrible apparition. Unwanted blood runs in my veins. Dark questions course through my body. One lives with one's fate. No, I haven't gained anything positive from the experience, not a bit of strength, nothing that might be useful to me in the future—nothing at all. There are organizations in Kigali that specialize in treating children in my situation, but I don't feel I need the comfort of psychologists and the like. I don't see any danger at home—I'm not afraid of being thrown out. It's just that a man may suddenly show up, someone I know would be harmful to my mama.

I DON'T KNOW if I can call myself Tutsi since I was born to an unknown father. My heart beats with the Tutsis. I stand with the people who have been ravaged by their memories. I feel like a survivor because I was born into turmoil. One way or another I really should have died. My best friends are survivors, because I feel calm with them. I'm not proud of being a survivor since I obsess about my birth. On bad days, bad thoughts lie in wait for me. I think that the way I came into the world was essentially shameful. Who wouldn't be shocked?

Even so, I can say that my mama is a Tutsi survivor and that I am very, very proud to be her daughter. It fills me with joy to be Claudine's daughter; it comforts me, too. A Tutsi gave birth to me, we share the same history, and I embrace it with all my heart. Some survivors claim they are cursed to be Tutsi. Myself, honestly, I wouldn't abandon my mother. I admire her, and that she gave me life even though the criminal forced her to stay with him in Congo for over a year! It's a miracle for a child—a human miracle. It has nothing to do with religion. Every day I owe Claudine my gratitude. She kept me when she returned while other mamas secretly strangled their children who had been conceived like me. It makes me happy and, I'd say, relieved as well. She was courageous to have accepted me as her beloved child despite the misfortunes she endured.

We love each other as mother and daughter in a way I don't have the words to describe. I admire her conduct in life. Do I ever ask myself questions about her? Plenty of times. How does she manage to control her feelings so as not to disappoint the people around her? How does she never lose her temper? I avoid asking her because I don't want to risk reviving her sorrow. I wonder how she can seem so calm regardless of the circumstances. Rumors don't disturb her, and she rules out revenge. She welcomes visitors into her home with a cheerful voice. She wakes up full of courage. Farming tires her out—that you can see—but she still laughs a lot as part of her nature. Her good spirits never leave her. I don't know why. She might get angry for a brief moment if I come home late, but she doesn't hold a grudge. It delights her to hear laughter in the house and at church. When she goes with me to Nyamata, we crack jokes and exchange smiles on our way and at the market. We have a great time, we share a juice. Basically, she encourages me to be happy.

At the very least, she won't let me wear out my arms in the field. My ambition is to become a nurse. And why not a nurse practitioner? I'm comfortable with biology and math. I know Claudine would have chosen nursing if she hadn't been caught up by the genocide. I'm going to put all my energy into nursing school. I'm enthusiastic about caring for people, in a public or private hospital. Being a teacher would please me, too. Nursing or teaching. Lots of professions are tempting, except for agriculture. Work in the fields runs you ragged. It causes swelling in your hands and feet.

NYAMATA IS BECOMING more and more modern thanks to the new electricity, televisions, and cars. The country is headed in the right direction because everywhere one looks they are building hospitals and banks and attractive boutiques. The new things we dig up on the internet don't frighten me. But modern times are wrecking the lives of simple people like farmers, who are going to be pushed out to the uncultivated land in the north. I think that with all the new construction, farmers' lives are bound to be uncertain. Am I going to marry a farmer? That would be fine if nobody else comes along. I'll try to avoid it.

I have a boyfriend, as I said. The same age as me, a student. He is medium height, even-tempered. His family is somewhat rich. We have been seeing each other for seven months. It's lasted. We like to share our personal feelings, but we don't bring up the future. I haven't met my future husband yet, though I do have an idea. A man who doesn't drink, who is decent height, neither fat nor skinny. It doesn't matter if he is rich as long as he is nice. Good manners are a must, and speaking well with the neighbors— never a harsh word. I would avoid someone brash. Why? He might come home drunk and make the house a mess and smack me around like that kind of man inevitably does. A Pentecostal would be best because that's what I am, and because Pentecostals don't drink alcohol. I could see a teetotaling Catholic as well. If my beloved isn't Christian, it all depends on how he behaves. It might be okay if he is very peaceful and nice. My parents will have to advise me on my choice. I lack experience, so there is the chance that I make a mistake about my suitor's behavior, that I overlook his mean traits. If I love a boy whom my mama rejects, forgetting him would be impossible, but leaving him, sure. I would have to, because Mama knows best. Could I marry against her wishes? Even if it makes me suffer a lot, I would accept her refusal out of respect.

I want to get married, raise a family—anywhere except in Kanzenze. It's no thrill getting married in the same place you have spent your childhood. Dark memories lurk down every path. You can't grow up, go to school, then get married on a hill, because too many know your secrets. In Kigali? Why not. It's a city—you see SUVs, huge comfortable houses with gates, and enticing boutiques. You can watch television. In town, people don't have their hands full with farming, and it's easier to get a lucky break than it is here.

I get bored in Kanzenze because young people lack amusing things to do. I would also like to meet new neighbors. I will bring two children into the world, and no more, so that I can feed and love them without excessive worries. I don't want any danger hanging over them. I won't tell them anything about my history, and I won't say a word about my anxieties. Unless they pester me for answers about the rumors they've overheard.

IDELPHONSE HABINSHUTI

NINETEEN YEARS OLD

Son of Fulgence Bunani, Hutu prisoner

IF MY PAPA HADN'T BEEN IMPRISONED, I WOULD have stayed in school. Today I'd be seeking my fortune somewhere other than on the river. That's the truth. My papa's fault has had a somewhat harmful effect on my character ever since I was a child. I don't pay attention to what I'm going to do. I'm never satisfied, and I lack conviction. I tend to change my mind. They say that I'm careless about things. That comes from all the work when I was young. First the war damaged my childhood goodwill. Didn't it force me to reflect on things more than a child born into a prosperous home? No, it hindered my intelligence. A comfortable life leads to exciting thoughts.

Without the killings, I'd be walking with the steps of a young man settled into a desirable job. I'd have married. I have a fourteen-month-old child named Kelia. Her mama's name is Olive; she lives in a *mudugudu*. She put the child in my hands because there was no chance of marriage. Her older brother demanded a dowry I couldn't pay. Then we quarreled about a fertile patch of land near the marshes he wanted to take for himself. He kept on about it for three months. In the end, the girl took her brother's side. If Papa hadn't returned to Rilima, she'd have decided in my favor. I don't regret it, because since then she has changed husbands three times, without even getting any land. But still.

I'll be careful the second time: I'll take up with a sensible girl who won't leave me with another baby on my hands. I'm going to look for a girl somewhere far from Kiganwa. When the betrothed live side by side, they can expect neither surprises nor novelty, only squabbles about land. One shouldn't be born, grow up, farm, and then get married in the same place. It's a dead harvest; you gain nothing new. I'd like to leave the Bugesera to start a new life without a past—in the Mutara, for example, where vast virgin pastures await the energy of new arrivals. I spoke to Papa about it in Rilima, without insisting too much. If he's released soon, I'll marry soon. If his time drags on, then obviously I'll have to be patient. Having a papa in prison would derail the negotiations between the families; it would disrupt the ceremonies. There's no use adding something unseemly to people's suspicions.

At school, I didn't sit at the front of the class like my brother, Jean-Damascène. I wasn't a dimwit, though. I was never reprimanded, I was never threatened in class. The teachers watched out for quarrels, even after our return from Congo. Outside class, it was a big thing, as I said. My goal? I longed to join the civil service, to wear the attire of a dignified civil servant, or to set up my own business as a craftsman. Anyway, the goal was to give up farming like a lot of Tutsi children have. It's understandable that things now favor the children of survivors. How so? They receive direct aid from the FARG, which pays the *minervals* at well-known schools. They go to boarding schools without even coming back to the hill on weekends. That's essential, because it's on the school bench that one learns to give up the hoe. Farm kids can't participate in the country's development like city children can—they're stranded on the unforgiving land. It's even worse if the parcel is supposed to be split up among siblings according to the new laws of inheritance that keep pouring down. Do I think about it a lot? About bad luck? Obviously, if Papa hadn't made mistakes in the marshes, I'd have my place on the school bench with my schoolmates. But I don't think that I'm paying my papa's debt to society. I'm paying for the misfortunes of society, which have wrecked my chances. I'm not the only one. Many children from the wrong ethnicity are penalized when their papas linger in prison.

Obviously, hearing about Papa's misdeeds makes me very unhappy. The killers' wickedness is beyond imagining. Honestly, those men cutting enough to break their own arms—who can explain it? Is it something a person my age can even understand? It's too much for us to accept such evil. Even still, I can't condemn my papa, since no one had an idle hand in the killings.

I LOVE MY PAPA. He gave me life. Every morning, I pray to God to come to his aid. If you see a young man in good health in front of you today, it's thanks to him. His strength courses in my veins. I don't want for food. He has watched over me despite the distance between us. I visit him once a month. Before it was on foot through the bush, but now I ride the bicycle he left. At Rilima, I present myself at the prison commissary to deposit some of the money I make from selling *urwagwa*, or fish. It's for Papa's canteen. We exchange superficial bits of news. He asks me about the parcel, he gives me advice for staking out the fields, he offers comforting words. No complaints about his sorry fate. He's friendly. He loves his children. A papa's attention makes up for everything they lack in life.

He's a strong man, neither tall nor short in stature, who has a taste for beans, of course, served with bananas, without wasting meat. He's upright, and he speaks well with the neighbors. There's never a quarrel except with a neighbor woman by the name of

Émilienne, when she stakes out the parcel on the sly, or when she drives her livestock through our sorghum. He holds no grudge against anyone. He looks through our notebooks to make sure that we are taking notes in class, and he checks the report cards at the end of the semester. Never mind that he isn't the fervent deacon he once was; he prays like everybody else. He likes selling *urwagwa* in his cabaret, and he knows how to make the land grow. If he hadn't suffered the misfortune of prison, really, I'd say we would have had a comfortable life and plentiful crops.

Ernestine's murder—I don't have all the right information to talk to you about it. My ears are closed to the neighbors' gossip. The only explanations that I'm waiting for are from my papa. What explanations do I hope that he'll give me? I don't know. A child doesn't want to hear everything from his papa. In 2010, the authorities summoned him to the *gaçaça* court, and he testified to his misdeeds, like they asked. The last day was a Sunday—he was lazing at home because he was racked with pain from his swollen feet. At nightfall, the court sentenced him to life in prison. It was the colleagues from his gang getting revenge. Why him if no one saw with their own eyes the killers slicing open Ernestine's belly? I can't get over that. I don't want to chase down rumors at the cabaret. If they pardon my papa, I'll ask him to take a moment to talk about what happened in the Ntarama church. I'll ask him questions without blame, because he has been punished enough.

My mama doesn't condemn my papa when she laments her solitude. Otherwise, you wouldn't see her astride the bicycle on her way to Rilima to visit him. She's a strong woman who gets on very well in farming. She's neither too skinny nor too heavy. Nevertheless, she suffers from stomachaches that curb her appetite for the usual food. She doesn't complain. She pays attention to her children and has replaced the mother of my little girl. The neighbors are full of appreciation for her because she's helpful. She's quick to lose her temper if someone provokes her, but it doesn't last for more than a brief moment. She just as quickly gives in with kind words. She doesn't get angry at her husband, like I said, never says a word about his mistakes. She loves him sincerely. She isn't the least neglectful, like other prisoners' wives who have given birth. Her courage hasn't left her; she's resilient even when the rains are late.

We don't quarrel. On the parcel, though, I've noticed that something is wrong. She sometimes drops the hoe, but not for a rest or a drink of water. She stands there motionless, thinking silently. The sun beats down on her face—she doesn't care. I can see that her thoughts have drifted to Rilima; they have carried away the worries of a woman abandoned by her prisoner husband. It's painful to watch. There really has been a decline because she has had to endure everything alone. She doesn't cry, she isn't motivated like before. She's waiting for God's mercy.

VINCENT AND JANVIER, Ernestine's brothers, I can't even go near, although we have known each other since childhood. Deep down, we don't want to acknowledge one another anymore. There's nothing to say—only the awkwardness of close neighbors. We aren't moved by friendship or memories of childhood games. If we happen to meet in a cabaret, one of us immediately leaves. In any case, I avoid talking about the genocide with children from the other ethnicity. Mentioning this dreadful past, even indirectly, puts you in an awkward position. Hutu and Tutsi children learn about the killings in completely different ways. If a Tutsi child is informed by his papa that his mama or grandmama was cut by a certain Hutu, that Hutu is never going to admit to his child that he cut the Tutsi woman. After twenty years, does anyone dare tell their children everything? Shame hangs over those who risk confiding in the wrong ethnicity, even if ethnicities have been abolished. When the wrongdoers confessed to the truth of wielding machetes, those were merely the confessions they gave in public at the *gaçaças*. They're wary of personal details.

I have Tutsi friends. We met on the school bench. Their families live in the *mudugudu* in Kiganwa. We talk a lot, we joke about soccer players who mess up their shots, we share shocking news we dig up on the internet. We discuss our concerns about farming when the rains are late. We avoid the genocide. We zigzag. Young people don't allow themselves to be affected by grumbling words, because if they did, their passions would compel them to fight. That would be the end of it. A small number opt for revenge because of their parents' misfortunes. They bury themselves in their resentment. It would be risky if a president were murdered again. On the other hand, many young people approve of the reconciliation policy. The atmosphere among young people doesn't breed hate like before. Hate has taken a step back. Things will start to sort themselves out.

I love Africa. It's a blessed continent, in my opinion. We don't encounter the world's racism here. Some nights, I listen to the agitated news from around the world on the radio. Here, I'm not afraid, though I keep on my guard. I'm glad of our fertile land for agriculture. I appreciate the climate when it doesn't play dirty tricks. In Kigali, new multistory buildings and SUVs are appearing every day. Twenty years from now, electricity and asphalt roads will stretch into the hills. Farmers will sell their land to go clear the bush in Tanzania. Not all the farmers will leave. In the distant hills, you'll still see people like us working the land with our hoes.

BESIDES THAT, I'm pleased with my health. I plug away working. I earn a bit. The Akagera River is where I put my zeal.

After his release from prison in 2003, my papa bought me a share in the fishing cooperative. A paternal cousin taught me the complex techniques for the nets and basket traps. Fishing is unpredictable. You waste a week without catching a big-caliber fish, and you're frustrated until the day comes when luck finds you and you haul in a fifteen-kilo carp. When you come away with nothing worthwhile, you're thrilled to get back to the parcel to harvest food. When you make a catch, you thank the river, which wears you out less than the land. I also look after the banana plantation, as I said. The *urwagwa* business doesn't disappoint. When you're short on one side, you draw from the other—it makes for a more balanced life.

The bloody catastrophe is in the past. Time heals. I like my hill in Kiganwa because I'm used to living here. We farm a fertile plot, an intensive banana plantation, and a plentiful river flows nearby. The food is good. But the climate plays so many tricks on farmers that they are no longer able to gauge the right time for seeding. In the past, they knew when the rain clouds were coming and going. Now rainfall is fickle, sometimes it skips a season. Three years ago, I managed to plant tomatoes. They paid off. Since then, drought has burned through two harvests. The meager rainfall means twice the number of trips for water. If you work unproductive land, you get annoyed and all you can think about is leaving.

Twenty years from now, I can see myself as the owner of a small business, with a motorcycle and a cow in the pen. The retail business is great. If you're frugal, the profits allow you to accumulate wealth. You don't waste time, you move ahead without the worries of farming. You become a businessman. Where will I go? Not to Kigali, which I don't know well enough to make a go of it. Expensive cities are dispiriting. I'll open a shop in the center of Nyarunazi for a start. Then I'll move to Nyamata or to Bicumbi, where my mother's family lives. They are close-knit like traditional families used to be. Would I move far away to forget everything? Has it crossed my mind? No, if you are born in a country, you have to accept its past. Here, though, I feel trapped by loneliness. Being a farmer separates you from others; being a prisoner's son separates you even more. I get bored, I struggle. I stumble and see that my life is wrecked to a certain extent. Basically, I don't wake up untroubled.

JEAN-DAMASCÈNE NDAYAMBAJE

SIXTEEN YEARS OLD

Son of Fulgence Bunani, Hutu prisoner

IT'S UNLUCKY TO BE THE SON OF A GENOCIDE killer. It's hard to explain, even to oneself. If the events hadn't soaked Rwanda in blood, life would have greeted me with kindly arms. Hearing that one's papa participated in awful crimes can be a harmful thing. My papa—he's mine; I love him more than anyone else. It's understandable. He's respectful of morals. The priest even chose him as deacon, because his education allows him to read the deep meaning of the Scriptures. His neighbors live with him in harmony. They get on well in conversation. He's very well considered because he shows himself reasonable whenever a dispute arises. No one gives him trouble. He doesn't weigh as much as a very muscular man, but his strength never fails him on the land. His *urwagwa* tastes good, and it's renowned. He's friendly, he doesn't cast evil looks. He's an upright man. The charges against him? Ernestine's murder? As I said, I don't know. Does a son try to investigate such terrible accusations?

My mama offers her kindness to everyone and still more to her children. She doesn't get angry with them, despite the pitfalls of life. She puts all her strength into the parcel. Wherever she goes, she's seen as an exemplary farmer, a woman who harvests a remarkable amount of crops without letting loneliness or drought slow her down. I get along well with her. We work in harmony at home, on the parcel, everywhere. We farm hand in hand to make up for Papa. Stomach ailments often trouble her, low spirits gnaw at her, too. She shows negative symptoms. When she can't see past a problem, she becomes overwhelmed, and she can't be helped. Loneliness overtakes her; she sulks. Do we mention it to her? She tells us that she isn't happy. She never blames Papa—she never utters a reproachful word against him—and she doesn't complain. She simply says that something about her isn't right.

The killers' misdeeds have caused long-lasting effects. But I don't think that being Fulgence's son will prevent me from finding a good wife, although it has pushed me into poverty. I don't lack for energy. I want to raise a big family later on. Who doesn't want that, even when you're penniless? A happy family cheered by children's games and sumptuous Sunday meals. I don't mix much with the girls from the hill since I haven't the time or spare money needed to charm them. That'll change. When I save up, I'm going to explore the streets of Nyarunazi or even Nyamata.

LATER ON, I hope to meet a girl who knows farming. Svelte or sturdy, her size doesn't matter, as long as she doesn't flinch from tackling the various kinds of work. A nice girl, pleasant with the neighbors, attractive, of course, and good at all that she does. Women of both ethnicities are just as capable regardless of the domain. In times past, this is what they said: In the fields, Hutus have the advantage of stronger biceps, because they eat food that gives them strength and energy. Tutsis, on the other hand, are better at tending livestock because they like to drink milk. We can't joke around about these things anymore, at least out loud, except with friends from the same ethnicity.

I live my life as a Rwandan first and foremost, like everyone else; or at least like all the Hutus who want to leave the past behind. We have to break with our bad reputation. We've also lived our share of misfortune. Which is why I don't attach any importance to having a Tutsi wife, provided that she doesn't hold my papa against me. As for my wife, I'd like her to be constructive, understanding of her husband, a teacher to the children, and, above all, to have adapted to modern life better than me.

If I were to win the national lottery, I'd go straight out and buy an immense parcel by the river. The land along the marshes overflows with promise: it's fertile and very valuable, especially since the rainy seasons have become such a torment. Forget about cows, which only add misery to one's worries. Sows, yes. I'd build a large farm. I've visited model facilities, with concrete floors lined with drainage ditches. Hogs get dirtier than cows—they have a nasty reputation—but twice a year they drop up to eight piglets. Can you imagine that? I'd open a construction supply business to take advantage of the country's development. And why not really learn computers and the internet like the young people my age? I'd build a house with a brick foundation where my family would live, with a veranda for selling *urwagwa*. I'd make my wife more beautiful so that she'd sing her joy to others.

This would be in central Nyamata, which is sure to be modern. Anyway, not far from there. In Nyamata, you already come across various shops. The prices at the market are decent. You see four-story buildings and streetlights when the electricity doesn't go out. The cabarets carry beer brands from Burundi and Kenya. It's not as modern as Kigali, but it's attractive nonetheless. You're among people you know, whatever the squabbles. It's a comfortable place.

If Papa hadn't gotten mixed up in the killings, I'd be studying math or economics. The teachers used to flatter me right in front of the other students' eyes. Life in a business suit and work in an office were what the future held. I don't see any chance of my dodging the consequences of the killings. Existence is bent on revenge up on the hills. There's absolutely zero chance of my becoming a car mechanic in a shop. An easy life has turned a deaf ear. God alone can hold out a kindly hand to me. I feel pessimistic. Poverty doesn't budge once it settles in. Yes, I believe that I suffer for my papa's wrongdoing. I work the hoe while friends turn the pages of textbooks at school. It makes me older than I am. I sometimes grumble about my papa. There's no lack of opportunities. Who could avoid it?

Despite all that, am I still hoping for a happier life? I think so—without knowing exactly the life to imagine, because I have already grown used to the hill. When fate has drawn a line for us, we become conditioned to follow it. We grow accustomed to the dark reputation of the genocide. I have carried the hoe down to the parcel since I was fifteen years old—do I have a choice? If God wanted me on the parcel, can I deviate from His plan? I don't know how to answer that.

But basically, any place that would take me away from Kiganwa, or even Nyamata, would be a kind of blessing.

ANGE UWASE

NINETEEN YEARS OLD

Daughter of Innocent Rwililiza, Tutsi survivor

MY MAMA WAS BEATEN IN AN ISOLATION CELL BY the *interahamwe*. They suspected her of colluding with the *inkotanyi* who were organizing at the border. This was before the killings. Her head still hurts. Their cruelty continues to torment her; she has been subjected to extraordinary suffering.

For seven weeks in Kayumba, my second papa scurried faster than forest prey. The hunt lasted nonstop from morning to night. A nasty wound damaged his leg. It's still there—he limps. In the climb up to Kayumba, he complains about the pain. I think their experiences encourage them to stand up for our family, to pass on our history better. Their difficulties give them strength and allow them to overcome their moments of weakness. Sometimes their troubles also drag them lower than grief. They're overwhelmed in every way. Their anxieties cause unpredictable behavior. You see them suddenly startled by a terrible memory. Their words rattle together. They're afraid, they're shaken up. We children understand, we're used to it.

I think that the genocide has brought me closer to my parents. How so? It's impossible to say. I'm also a survivor, despite my young age. The survivors hold on to everything they've endured.

As a family, we try to support one another more than others do. But even so, I'm pretty sure that my parents don't understand me any better. They aren't any more tolerant. No, no, they aren't any more understanding or any smarter about my adolescent up-bringing. They don't see my friends with a kinder eye. My little quirks don't make them smile. Not one bit. They watch over me with the strict severity of their generation. They believe in their adult ideas. They simply offer more kindness in difficult times.

THE IDEAL HUSBAND? He'd be Rwandan. Why? Would a foreigner understand me? Would a man who hasn't known the threat of the machete accept my timid personality? If he sees that my torments upset the picture of a model wife, he might heap criticism on me. Sometimes I feel tempted to leave to study abroad. To Canada, where my mother's family is scattered. Or Australia, another destination, because I have heard that calm people live there, the climate is good, and universities welcome foreigners without any trouble. But my husband, I also want him to be Tutsi. I won't say a survivor, but still a Tutsi, so that we get along in every situation.

I hope that he is educated, tall in stature, because I myself am very tall and slender. That he talks with the neighbors without seeming awkward or aggressive and that he doesn't mistreat a soul. He doesn't look for a drink every night, he listens to me so that he can lavish me with comforting words. He doesn't force me into intimacies, like so many others do. He doesn't give orders by bullying. I won't go looking for him by myself, outside the traditional customs of the family, but I will decide. If the suitor doesn't satisfy my parents, they will have to tell me why. For instance, if they think he cheats and hides ill will in his heart, I will hear them out. Then I will make my own decision whether to love him or leave him.

I don't think about it very much because first I want to get a good diploma. I enjoy my studies. I was accepted into the history-economics-geography combination. I feel at ease with economics. I am confident that I'll gain the right number of points for university. My ambition is law school, the judiciary. Being a judge appeals to me. I'd practice my profession in Nyamata because Nyamata makes me happy. I couldn't live my whole life on the hills, since I'm wary of the customs of the countryside. They set their traps. The hoe wears you out all year-round, and all the worries that go with it. I also fear the mentality, the gossip, the backwardness of family planning that women have to endure, in addition to the other drudgery. Nyamata is up-to-date, worry-free.

In my dreams for the future, I have never turned my back on our Bugesera hills. I have never imagined myself in a country without genocide, because it's something that I grew up with. Who wants to cast off their childhood? To forget their precious family and ancestors? Not for a minute have I wanted to leave my memories behind. Can you sort out the good from the bad of your existence? That yields only disappointments and delays one's fate. I'm glad to be Rwandan and Tutsi. That's how I have always seen myself. The future is all that I could wish for.

IMMACULÉE FEZA

SIXTEEN YEARS OLD

Daughter of Innocent Rwililiza, Tutsi survivor

I'M GLAD I WAS BORN IN A FAMILY OF SURVIVORS because I would have suffered in a Hutu family. Many Hutus had a hand in evil; they're seen as harmful. Their presence is no longer valued among us. Friendship no longer greets them with joyful cheers at their neighbors' doors. I'm not a survivor like my sister Ange, who was born before the machetes. As the younger sister, I try to imitate her. I copy her styles and skin care, I keep an eye on the smiles she sneaks at boys, I take over her things—everything except her experience as a survivor. She was the target of machetes, not me. She heard the death cries. I didn't hide out in a false ceiling, prayers trembling on my lips. Survivors stopped at nothing to live, and many now fear that others have lost respect for them for what they had to do. They lived in terror and filth; above all, they knew they were abandoned. You can tell that deep down a shameful secret blocks their hearts. Myself, I grew up in peace and quiet, but in a certain way I feel somewhat like a survivor, because that secret surrounded my childhood. It's still there in the house.

Does that worry me? I have no idea, since I don't know if it has tainted my future happiness. When my papa and mama speak of their loved ones cut by the machetes, it reminds me that their loved ones would also have been mine. Survivors recount the deaths in the marshes in order to make a place for the dead in their memories. Remembering is so important to them because it gives life to the dead. We children can offer our parents only kindness in return. So I give a double dose.

Survivors' memories filled my childhood. The thought of forgetting the dead upsets me as much as it does an actual survivor. No, it doesn't bother me to have inherited that—why would it? Sometimes I get angry. I despise the people who caused so much pain. I picture ways of taking revenge on the murderers. When I was a child, I hoped to see them lined up and shot on the hill. I wanted to put them to death myself. But time has inspired more sensible thoughts in me; scolding had its effect. Children cannot avenge their parents if their parents aren't considering it themselves. We can't kill contrary to their wishes. That doesn't prevent feelings like ill will from smoldering deep down within us at times. I also know that our country is calling on all our strength to help provide enough to eat, especially now that the droughts have begun to come ahead of schedule.

Basically, I don't know what to say. Do I think about forgiveness? That is a tricky question for a girl with so much kindness around her. What good would it do me to forgive? Who would I forgive? What importance would my forgiveness have in the eyes of others? I am neither an orphan nor a trauma victim. Can my forgiveness mean as much as it would coming from my parents or my sister Ange? Or from a girl left alone with her terrible memories? I haven't had to struggle against poverty like a girl stuck on a barren piece of land.

I'm proud of my parents; they survived the blades. Still, I notice strange things in their behavior. Their unpredictable moods, which change for no apparent reason. For example, you ask them a question and they don't respond; instead, they sulk, obviously thinking of something else. My papa walks with a limp due to his injury; he comes to a halt between two steps, then cracks a joke at his own expense, which no one understands. My mama suffers from migraines; her mind isn't right because of them. She speaks to us in a gentle tone of voice, then suddenly goes out into the courtyard alone. We can tell that she's stopped paying attention to anyone around her, that her thoughts have drifted elsewhere. If she says something, her meaning escapes us. Sometimes Papa stays in bed late. Mama tells us he mustn't be disturbed while his memories plague him. If it hadn't been for the genocide, a more frivolous childhood would have brought me steadier parents, smiling grandparents, as I already said, and a prosperous plot in Kibungo, where we would have had plenty of bananas and milk. We would have passed around drinks at loud family gatherings. We would have sung ourselves hoarse after Sunday meals. Rwandan traditions would have ensured our happiness. The world would have showed us a more pleasing face. But I am not unhappy with my Tutsi fate.

It's daunting for a little girl, but it's nothing disastrous. I definitely feel Tutsi. I grew up in a family of Tutsis. I have heard their story from my earliest childhood. It binds me to them. The loved ones lost in the killings, the pursuits they endured in the forest, the fright they had in their hideouts—what I have learned obliges me to take good care of my parents. Loss has surrounded my youth. Children born after the genocide won't ever know what it was like for those who watched the raised machetes. They never saw the blades. Myself, I'm not gnawed by anxiety, I've never been struck with panic. The dead make me sad. Hearing about them doesn't shock me because I've been told about them with sympathetic words. I miss them. The dead impose a view of the living world that children in faraway countries cannot share. Which is why I spend all the time I can with Tutsi friends who understand my story. Even if they sometimes appear traumatized.

Hearing the fear in various accounts of the genocide prevents me from ever completely trusting others. That's the attitude that the dead have imparted. It's a lesson. In every situation, you keep some room for yourself—a haven, so to speak, only for you. You hold back your impulse to trust. You can't freely confide in your best friend for fear that she might repeat things that lead to arguments. It ruins your life. When a genocide sweeps through your childhood, you come out cautious and somewhat timid. Whether from Tutsis or Hutus, the threat of betrayal gnaws at you. Jesus foresaw that Peter would betray him three times and Peter didn't miss a one. It's a warning from God: human beings are capable of betrayal at any time. Myself, I pray for God to deliver us from this fear in order to restore our calm happiness. I like to pray and to feel free. That means living a normal life without extraordinary conflict. I'm wary of things that rouse worries in my head. That's why I try to have a good time, and I hang out with girlfriends.

I HOPE TO continue my education in Butare. The climate there seems neither too hot nor too cold. Regular rains wash away the dust. The university is supposed to be international. I am leaning toward biology, maybe to become a nurse or veterinarian. I am going to move to a huge city where there are booming stadiums for seeing soccer and parks for winding down. I am thrilled by charming conversations and places to dance. I also have the ambition of becoming a journalist. I think that journalism would be less difficult than other subjects. Journalists are like famous people—they're well-known and in good health. They have polished manners; they appear pleasant on television. International journalists travel in search of information, crisscross faraway countries, and deal in new ideas. They discover surprising customs—that's what I would like to do.

I feel impatient for marriage, of course. I don't want grand nuptials, full of pomp and posh guests. What's the use? My husband? I would like him to be tall in stature, the same age as me, and, the most important thing, nice. A boy a little bit rich, though, so he can provide for a family living in a baked-brick house. He could be a lawyer or mayor, for example. Anyway, a man who is capable of checking with me before he acts. He should like to joke with his wife and exchange kind words with her. A farmer, that could work, too, since Rwandan land feeds its population. But only if he is a well-to-do farmer with a decent number of cows, employs farmhands, and plants more than just beans, so we aren't as vulnerable to poor harvests. I wouldn't want anything to do with a husband who isn't peaceful, with a disruptive presence in the family. Let him go drink with his pals at the cabaret, but not so much that he gets drunk. He can come from any region—that doesn't matter to me.

Except not a Hutu. What if he's kind and understanding? No, no, not a chance, because they have committed too many terrible things against us. No, I wouldn't accept a very handsome Hutu, wealthy, polished, a dandy, even, because his presence might upset my parents. Knowing what they lived through during the killings—and my big sister Gigi, too—it would be shameful for me to bring a suitor from the other ethnicity into the family. Not out of fear of the person but because of the lack of respect for my people. And distrust: mine of him and his of me. Distrust is fatal to one's love. A family that has experienced the machetes is forever made fragile, more cautious.

The time of carefree young people is over; we'll never talk to one another again without awkwardness and lies. Nowadays, we return to our side every time the genocide gets mentioned. We don't dare poke fun at one another like people do in comedies. I don't know if we will eventually understand one another. I don't think my Hutu friends' parents talk about their lives the way mine do. The papas mask their misdeeds from their children's eyes, and the mamas use words to disguise the truth about the papas' wickedness. They refuse to stand as they are, as shameful wrong-doers. Even when they blurt out a confession, it never follows a straight line. Their children aren't all made the same way, though. Certain Hutu children provoke their parents. Others adjust to their parents' lying—they give in or play with the truth themselves for the love of family.

Deep down, a lot of young people from both ethnicities con-ceal a desire for revenge. That's why so many young Rwandans are religious. They put their trust in God in order to alleviate their sorrows, in order not to stumble. They know that prayers and songs soften the anxieties that arise from the terrible events. The huge modern world decreases children's gloom and, of course, their anxiety, too. Young people surf the internet, many take off abroad and speak English. We dance to electronic music. Even so, in twenty generations, young Tutsis will still think about the time when their ancestors were almost exterminated. Myself, I don't see starting a family with just anybody. I won't hide a single detail of my parents' history from my children. I hope that my children will do the same because so many fears mustn't fall into oblivion. We're keeping on our guard, since the threats are quiet for now.

THE HISTORY OF the genocide isn't unbearable. It affects me; it's part of who I am. I don't want to be relieved of the sadness that comes from being a survivors' daughter. I'm not hoping to be rid of it by leaving the country. I feel free when I take walks with my brothers and sister and visit with friends. I like school and kidding around. I never get tired of dancing, and looking through the shops is a delight. The hair salons and dance halls are the only places I avoid. They can be risky. Why? Conceiving before marriage. The market never gets old—I'm surrounded by happy faces. I am always eager to see the clothes from Kigali shown off by the shopkeepers. The market is mindless fun. We love meeting up in various spots with different people; we tease one another with friends we meet. I don't feel that Nyamata holds me back. Although Kigali is tempting, too. I go there sometimes with the choir or to keep Mama company at the hospital. We stop in at the cabaret to order a Fanta soda. In Kigali, people live in comfort, and the shop windows have fancy displays. It thrills your curiosity to discover new things. One is constantly learning about the world's surprises. It's chaotic—wanting too much is risky—but that's our capital.

FABIOLA MUKAYISHIMIRE

NINETEEN YEARS OLD

Daughter of Joseph-Désiré Bitero, Hutu prisoner

WHEN I WAS FOURTEEN, I SAW MY PAPA LEAVE FOR the penitentiary. My mama did her best to shoulder more of the work, but Papa proved impossible to replace. I cherish him as a daughter cherishes her papa, but I know him only through the fleeting words we manage to exchange in the Rilima courtyard.

When you're a young child, you enjoy yourself whatever you do, even doing nothing at all. But with a papa in prison, a little girl isn't doted upon as she ought to be; she misses out on strolls seated atop his shoulders and his extraordinary tales at evening gatherings. She doesn't chitchat like other children do. She's on the alert before she even knows why. Every word carries risks. To be safe, she copies what she hears from the lips of adults. Infants don't suffer so much from being different; they don't feel worse off since they don't know how other children live. In adolescence, though, one feels frustrated not being able to go along with friends. One yearns to play, to clown around carefree, and to cut loose with the group—going dancing at the cabaret on Saturdays, having fun listening to music and whiling away the time with the boys. Since I became an adolescent, I feel like I'm looked upon negatively, even if I see myself as pretty. I stay withdrawn, I seem shy for my age.

I have been dismissed from school numerous times because of money, which means that I won't finish high school until I am twenty years old. I have had to take on odd jobs on the weekends while my girlfriends were teasing each other with the boys.

My personality has changed because of it—the way I think, anyway. If it hadn't been for the war, my papa would be settled in comfortably among us at home. Maybe I would have gone to a private school, and I'd be sitting proudly on the class bench at the National University. I'd be living in a solidly built house like our old one in Gatare. I'd wake up joyful and pick out a pretty dress. Yes, I feel my papa's reputation has held me back.

SINCE I'VE BEEN at boarding school, I go to visit my papa during school vacations. When nostalgia overwhelms me, I return on weekends if I find enough to pay the bus fare. All our visits make me happy. He's nice. He always wears a smile when we meet, and he finds the right words. I see him as a strong, a very strong man, and good. He's intelligent, of course, which explains why he was named president of the Youth Movement. He's cheerful, as I said. We boost each other's spirits. When I am there with him, I feel content, then suddenly anxiety sets in. My heart sinks as soon as I think of leaving him. He jokes around, but I can tell that he's hiding his true feelings from me: when the guards end our visits, his mind lingers, and you can see that he'd like to sneak more time—he puts off our goodbyes. His face shows signs of anger, but he conceals it with false cheer.

I have always seen him as a caring man who loves his daughter. Everyone respects him in Rilima, even the guards. He's someone who inquires after everyone no matter who it is. He never mentions his pain from arthritis. He gives sensible advice. Prison has put him back on the path to goodness. Why would an intelligent, cheerful man one day turn toward such a dreadful fate? Why did he make the wrong choice? I can't say. It's troubling. I don't know what acts my father committed. Deep down, I'm not eager for details. I don't go digging for the truth in his absence. I'm not anxious to find out.

My mama defends my papa against the most serious allegations, but of course there are plenty of opportunities for her to complain. She laments our lost comfort. She grumbles that Papa's ruinous politics brought misfortune into our home. She acknowledges that Papa, as a ringleader, should be punished, but that he shouldn't have to endure more than the men who nearly broke their arms swinging the machetes. I don't know, myself. How could I? Should I believe the people who say the worst? I think my papa fully supported Habyarimana's nasty policies. No one forced him. The advantages of the situation drew him in.

The question of why he did what he did upsets me, because it's beyond me to say. Can a young girl really fathom her papa's soul? The whole story eats away at me. It can feel dirty being the daughter of someone charged with a crime. One suffers for the sins of others. It's difficult. It's tricky to talk about. Anyway, who is going to listen? There are neighbors all around who mourn their lost relatives. I dread talking about it, I prefer not to have to argue to defend my papa. What good are arguments? I avoid enemies.

If a presidential pardon were to open the iron gates for my papa, joy would welcome him home. There would be no chiding from us—he's our papa, after all. We would celebrate, although not something grandiose like a traditional celebration. We'd keep it simple because of the neighbors' eyes. We'd give thanks to God and express our deep gratitude to the authorities. We'd have a wonderful time and prepare an amazing meal. Would his return go smoothly? I think we'd all have to adapt. Getting used to a father's rule at home would be a real transformation, since we children grew up in a way that isn't easy to change. Our daily existence of struggling "by hook or crook" against poverty and shame without a papa's authority has made us stick very close together.

If he leaves prison, I will ask him about his life there, how he spent his time with his fellow prisoners, and how he turned to God. Would I criticize him for preventing us from having a comfortable childhood in a well-regarded neighborhood in Nyamata? I don't know. Would I ask him what he himself did during the killings? That would be impossible—too disrespectful. Would I ask him if he wielded the machete? That would throw us back into a terrible past. It would be disruptive; it would undermine the family.

A genocide is more than a lesson. There are plenty of questions a prisoner's daughter asks herself—about the war, human wickedness, ancestral disputes. She struggles more than friends born to comfortable families. From an early age, she becomes accustomed to death. A young girl from a family without worries encounters death in the faces of old age and sickness. It's something accidental—it becomes natural death, if I can put it that way. Among us, we experienced a death by machete blades, and it makes us endlessly afraid. What has it taught us? To overcome disappointments despite everything, not to get discouraged so easily. In a quiet family my thoughts would have flowed untroubled, but in my family the situation is a bit chaotic. I have had to figure things out intellectually.

IN THE FUTURE, I imagine being a manager. I like economics and economics likes me, since our exams have earned me good grades. I am hoping for a national scholarship, which will depend on the number of points I score on my exams. A degree in management or business administration from the university in Kigali would be a good fit for me. I want to live in the capital and not end up in a country job.

I'm passionate about music, especially Beyoncé, zouk, and American and Rwandan songs, of course. I'm a fan of Tom Close and King James, like everybody else. Miss Shanel, too, because she's alluring. I don't go in for Congolese music—it's too wild and, furthermore, vulgar. I don't dance anymore. I used to dance during my first years of high school. Now dancing makes me uncomfortable. I consider myself too old at almost twenty to go out dancing with fifteen- or sixteen-year-olds at the Cultural Center. Why? It wouldn't be respectable for me to be seen waiting for a sixteen-year-old boy to ask me to dance.

In Nyamata, the young people my age like to party, especially at Black and White. You meet a lot of boys whom you get to know and joke around and dance with. But a dance band requires nice dresses and shoes, and not everyone can afford fancy pumps for dancing on a Saturday night. Do I have admirers who would spend their money on me? Am I sometimes asked out because of my looks? No. Who would invite me? No one invites me. Parties are something young rich kids worry about.

If I were to win the raffle one day, I would visit all the boutiques. No, first I would hire masons to build a brick house for my mama. I would put a big-screen TV in the living room so we could watch the Rwandan and Kigali teams, because the Kigali club plays a marvelous game of soccer. Not to mention the Champions League teams. Then I would buy myself dresses and shoes, like the young people my age, and a smartphone, obviously.

Africa has nothing more to prove, because its riches are beyond compare. I admire African culture, its beauty. On the other hand, Africans don't always appreciate one another as they should. They give in to harmful influences. That's what I have learned in class, anyway. The teachers also say that, twenty years from now, Rwanda will be developed enough to take care of its entire population. We young people are going to have to choose how to live as neighbors—in other words, to choose between bitter words and mutual support. Our future? I don't know. The threat of massacres hangs over the hills. But I still don't believe in any curse.

Myself, in twenty years' time, I hope to be a wife with a family that is very well provided for. Marriage is bound to be a bit awkward because of my papa. Who is going to take care of the dowry or walk with me arm in arm to the altar? I'll be patient. It all depends on encounters one can't predict. Still, I'm looking for a husband who offers love willingly, who doesn't force, and who doesn't prevent his wife from feeling modern: a man who is truly emancipated thanks to his understanding of the wider world, and more knowledgeable than farmers about new inventions. Catholic or Pentecostal, his religion makes no difference as long as he shows himself to be as heartfelt as other people in his beliefs. Anyway, a man who can tell good from evil, who won't be tempted by the devil's tricks. Also, a man who is well-to-do.

Could I marry a Tutsi boy? Being honest isn't easy. Marriage demands a deep understanding between the two partners, and it means Hutu and Tutsi families living with what happened. In any case, personally, I want to sweep the past far away from my children's innocent steps—no troubles to dampen their adolescent joy. I refuse to let them get tripped up by hurtful rumors. If I fall in love with a Tutsi boy, that would be fine with me. As things are, neither my mama nor my papa could possibly object. But how would the boy's family react? They might complain, refuse to overcome the past, and give me dirty looks.

I definitely feel Hutu. Hutus feel uncomfortable with the name, but not me. People say that Hutus used to live together stalwart and proud before the genocide. They claimed to be the strongest. Now it's the Tutsis' turn to act that way. People say that Hutus used to farm the land as bold and skillful farmers while the taller Tutsis showed themselves especially shrewd in raising animals. Nowadays, "Hutu" and "Tutsi" are words that ring out "danger" to the ears; the terms have been banned in schools. But ethnicity was manipulated on all sides—yes, on all sides. We aren't supposed to talk about ethnicity anymore, although no one is willing to give up their own. Can Hutus erase their Hutu misfortunes? Can Tutsis forget what they have had to endure because they are Tutsi? Future generations won't forget a thing, in my opinion, however hard they try to put the past behind them. That's why I've got nothing more to say on the subject. I call myself Rwandan, which is enough for me.

BASICALLY, in twenty years' time, I would like to be living in Italy. I have heard that they live in peace and quiet, with no ethnicities or machetes. It's a country with no greed and no religious wars, unlike everywhere else in the world. The Italians revere the pope, who watches over them with love from the balcony of Saint Peter's. Good cheer infuses everything Italian—that would be a delight. Are the pizzas tasty? I don't know. Anyway, I wouldn't miss beans. If I'm lucky enough to find a good job there, I'll get used to the way of life. They say that in Italy people outdo each other trying to be the most stylish.

FABRICE TUYISHIMIRE

TWENTY-TWO YEARS OLD

Son of Joseph-Désiré Bitero, Hutu prisoner

TWENTY YEARS FROM NOW, NOTHING WILL SET ME apart from others. I don't know if people will forget about my father. Me, I'll be a man like anyone else with no more worries than any of them. I'll have a successful family. I would have no problem promising my love to a Tutsi girl as long as she doesn't cut corners with the housework. Charm has nothing to do with family origins. If her parents expressed their disapproval, too bad for them. In any case, mine wouldn't have a single angry word to say against our nuptials.

I don't know yet about my profession. The family curse has put a school diploma out of reach. Now I want to get a license to drive a bus-taxi—or a truck, which is my preference. Unfortunately, the cost of the exam requires a small windfall. As I told you, I get by with odd jobs, but the money flows straight to the family. I haven't put any under the mattress for the moment.

My hope is to be a long-distance truck driver. I dream of trips on asphalt roads that take me far away. Driving a truck would get me involved in the economic boom that has been transforming our country. I'd reap my little share of the profits. Twenty years from now, I don't see myself rich the way I would have been

without the misfortunes of the war, but I still see a man relatively well-to-do. That hope hasn't left me. I cling to it come
what may. I'll live in Kanazi or Nyamata, or somewhere else if I
earn more. I'll drive long semi-trucks on routes all the way to
Dar es Salaam or Mombasa. I'll sleep with my bundle of things
in the cab, I'll bend my ear to the sounds of the engine, I'll grease
the U-joints. I'm fond of long-distance trucking. To Congo? Why
not. I'm not afraid of returning to the Masisi, of transporting
merchandise to Kisangani or all the way to the capital. I'm fond
of Africa. We have a favorable climate without the ordeal of icy
winters. On the internet, they show all kinds of cataclysms in the
world. You see nuclear earthquakes in Japan, terrorism and the
like. War is less of a threat in Africa. The land offers its riches for
farming. It's a gift for the inhabitants, even for people like me who
turn to other things. Despite everything, we're guided by an en-
viable fate.

WHEN WE WERE children, our mama would talk to us about
our papa. She told us about our happy family before the war, how
people appreciated him as a teacher, how his reputation spread
throughout the district. She described the good life in Gatare.
Does she lament the bad decisions? She doesn't speak in that
way. She doesn't regret having stayed by my father's side during
the killings. She can't imagine a wife in conflict with her husband.
Whenever drought closes in, she takes to complaining about her
lot. Sometimes her mind grows agitated, and she grumbles about
Habyarimana's machinations. Yet I have never heard her blame
my father for getting involved. She feels the loneliness of a
woman farming her parcel alone. She's plagued by headaches,
which sometimes force her to the clinic. She doesn't hold Papa

responsible. She repeats out loud that he never cut anyone with
his blade.

If Papa is still in prison, it's because he led the *interahamwe*
in his van. But I still believe that the court went too far when it sentenced him to death. People say that reconciliation holds the
future of the country in its hands. Twenty years in prison would
have been fairer, then a pardon, like so many of his associates received, so that he could return to the love of his family. Would I
like to say something about the charges against him? No, because
I can't know the truth without hearing it from him. How can a son
swallow whole the words of those who accuse his father of raising
his machete or firing his gun without listening to him first? My
criticisms will have to wait for his explanations. I don't go digging
around in his past. Questioning neighbors or his old colleagues
would be disrespectful. Only a father's truth can convince the son.
When someone has given you life, no one can harm him in your
eyes as long as he is away.

When odd jobs earn me a little money, I rent a bicycle and I
bring him news and hygiene products. Sometimes I take Fabiola
or my mama along. It's a forty-kilometer trip. Papa and I talk about
family life, how things are going with all the difficulties in life.
We count off the little brothers and sisters. He insists that we look
over the schoolwork and scolds the ones who haven't kept up. He
encourages me to redouble my efforts. To find a well-paying job
so that the family can live in a sturdier place than our earth-and-
sheet-metal home. He shrugs if someone brings up the situation
in Rwanda. He doesn't mention his court case anymore. We exchange bits of news about acquaintances. He describes how he
has entrusted his fate to God, and he recommends that we
put our trust wholeheartedly in Him, as he never fails to do each
and every day. Sometimes we say nothing; we're content simply

looking at each other. There's too much hubbub around us. Time presses.

If, by the grace of God, he's freed, I'll ask him questions. Maybe I'd explain to him that I've suffered the consequences of his past and that I'd like to know who the instigators of the killings were. How it was all planned out. Am I sure? No, it would all depend on how he is. Would I insist that he give me details? No, it might be repugnant to listen to. You get burned by touching certain wickedness. If he told me that he never killed, I'd accept his answer, because I don't know a single neighbor who came forward with any proof of a murder that my father committed.

If my papa decided not to answer my questions, I would feel indignant inside. If he said that after having endured all these years in prison he no longer wanted to be mixed up in the past, I know it would disappoint me. I'm still eager to have certain truths. Would I contradict him? He's the person I should venerate the most, after God. Can a son blame his father to the point of turning his back on him forever? When a child stands before his father, he feels too intimidated to sort out the good qualities from the bad, especially if that father has been held behind bars from the boy's earliest years.

MY CHILDHOOD DIDN'T leave me carefree, like other children were. Anyway, my particular experiences have had only harmful consequences on my personality. I'm sure of it, I have gained nothing good from this, nothing to pass on to my descendants. I don't know what kind of person I would have become. I would have gotten a school diploma. I would have been comfortable showing off among my friends. Bugesera FC would have handed me a jersey and cleats. I would have worn a smart gray suit to the wedding ceremonies that neighbors invited me to. Does being my father's son now help me to choose a better path? Does it strengthen me to face the future? How could it possibly? There is nothing worth learning from this kind of experience. No, not a single useful lesson for the human spirit. Except for distrust and shame. Compared with ordinary children, I've come out of this without having gained a thing.

SANDRA ISIMBI

EIGHTEEN YEARS OLD

Daughter of Édith Uwanyiligira, Tutsi survivor

WHEN I WAS A CHILD, I WAS ALWAYS HAPPY TO lend a hand with the housework. We never stopped singing in the courtyard. At night, we gathered around the table. Mama waited for each of us to describe our day. Then she asked us to correct what we hadn't done right in the future and to seek forgiveness for those we had offended. She told us that we didn't have to pray, but that we should do so whenever we liked, to give thanks to God, for example, for all that we had.

Myself, I like to pray early in the morning. Why? I don't know. And at night in bed, to fall asleep like a little girl. Mama's kindness has given me stability. I haven't been plagued by disappointments or any terrible hardships. I have never felt the need for psychological support like so many other survivor children. As soon as Bertrand and I were big enough to head down the road to school, Mama began inviting all the little neighborhood children to play in our yard. They kept her entertained the whole day long and gave her comfort in her solitude. There was always a crowd of kids at our place.

Mama taught us to share everything. We were very, very joyful. If food was lacking, good cheer took its place. In the first years, we had no idea how much energy we demanded of her. It brought back her longing for Papa, who was no longer present, as he should have been, to add his strength to hers. But her will never wavered, and her mood was always bright. The children provoked her with the silly things they did, and she paid them back with laughter.

Everyone was fond of hearing her describe her childhood and her loving family, especially how alluring she was as a young girl. How, during vacations, her grandparents overflowed with the desire to spoil her. The celebrations for which she dolled herself up, the parties spent with girlfriends sharing embroidery, and all the tales that people told to please her. She recalled the innocent kisses with Papa, whom she had dearly loved since school, and their wedding as an elegant young bride and groom—and we laughed. We were glad to hear the joyful memories of a family the machetes hadn't taken from us yet.

She talks about my papa in words of happiness, about his preferences, his manly quirks, his tall stature, his always-steady gestures, and his upright bearing, for which he was respected. I know that he showed himself to be strong and kind with his acquaintances. She doesn't dwell on things; she recounts in passing. Occasionally, if we happen upon a soccer game, she describes how he played captain, for example, adding new details about his life, or their Sunday bike rides or walks in the forest. She doesn't overdo it so as not to sharpen her regret.

I don't know if the genocide has brought my mama and me closer. A genocide destroys everything, family ties included. Do survivor families have deeper bonds because of their shared experience? What bonds are there with those who are absent? A void divides the families who have suffered. The memory of the dead drives them apart. Each member feels lonelier than the next. At school, when I hear classmates describe vacations with their grandparents, it tears at my heart.

Grandchildren are only too happy to chat with their grand-parents, who offer encouragement and kind advice. Grandparents tell tales from long ago, and they dote on you because you're the delightful child they no longer have. At vacation time, I'm seized with sadness knowing that I have no family to welcome me else-where or to offer surprises to my eyes. Sometimes it's the despair of not being able to play on my papa's lap. The feeling doesn't linger, though, because Mama chases it away. I have wanted for nothing that a mother can provide. She has understood me and given me all that I have needed. Mama is devout. She never gets angry without a reason, she doesn't quarrel, and she spares no kindness toward visitors to her home. She lavishes advice on her children to help them solve their problems. Obviously, she can't hide the obsessions of a survivor, but she puts on a very, very cheer-ful face. Laughter sweeps our family's sadness away.

I AM TUTSI. My parents are Tutsi. I have inherited their ethnic understanding. They experienced Tutsi history starting with the pogroms of the 1960s. I belong to that history, and I'll continue it whatever the authorities decide about ethnicities. I am both happy and unhappy about my ethnicity and I'll explain why. It pains me because my people were hunted down like prey. My father was killed, my mother has suffered heartbreak and humili-ation as a Tutsi. You take no pride in misfortunes unless you are the one giving chase. On the other hand, my ethnicity makes me glad because otherwise I'd have to be Hutu. I thank God that I didn't inherit a wicked heart, a heart driving me to hunt Tutsis, to wade in mud past my knees, pushing me to seek their extermina-tion. Being hunted is more humane than blackening your soul in the hunt.

I was born into a brutal life that children from peaceful countries will never know. How could my understanding of human nature be the same as theirs? In the past, ethnicities shared a carefree existence. Suspicion now lurks in everyone's soul. Cutting down neighbors in front of their families is such an extraordinary act that it weighs on people's minds forever. Such crimes are impossible to understand, so we keep on our guard. I don't tremble in fear of being killed when I see Hutu neighbors; I'm not afraid of the machetes the farmers carry home from the fields. And yet I know that all the promises might not be kept. When people have lived in animal filth, the memory never leaves them. Neither the vicious hunters nor their victims are safe from the grudges that are quietly reemerging.

I see history as something chaotic because people tell it in different ways. One ethnicity chooses words that follow a straight line, the other zigzags. A Hutu papa can't sit with his son to tell him about the people he carved up with his machete. He has every reason not to confess his actions, because the child would shudder at the thought of sleeping in the same home. Or the opposite would happen: if the child is a boy, he would dream of imitating his papa out of a sense of pride, so that his papa would value and compliment him.

I plan on talking with my children without passing over any of the details of our fate. The barbaric incidents, too, if they ask me. You have to anticipate a child's fear. You have to tell him about the past before he becomes suspicious of life. Not all survivors think so. Many shield their children from certain truths that they consider reprehensible—for example, surviving in place of a relative. They hope to prevent their children from telling their grandchildren. It's a tricky business. If a child notices that too many things aren't right around him, he is liable to go off sulking alone—if he has never met his grandmama, for example, or if he sees how sad his grandpapa is. If he notices sudden silences at family gatherings, he is liable to worry and behave badly. He might stop paying attention in class, neglect his chores, or smoke cannabis. To grow up feeling safe, you have to tell him. The worst thing for a child is hearing about his parents' misfortunes or misdeeds from the neighbors' lips. The child comes away distrustful, or disgusted. Suspicion breeds spite.

ILLNESS, THE DOCTORS SAY, was waiting for me at birth. Even still, I didn't get the care I needed in time. That's because of our dreadful existence during the killings, the frantic escape into the bush, and the miserable years that followed. I remember having terrible attacks when I was five years old. I had just started elementary school, and they kept at me through the end of every semester, meaning that I had to redo my first year. Mama put me in the care of traditional healers, but my illness fooled even them. We stood in line for visits at the clinic, and the doctors diagnosed the disease and prescribed nonstop medication. I was often hospitalized. I enrolled at a learning center whose classes worked better for me. I made it to high school with nothing worse than being a year behind.

I wanted to follow in my brother Bertrand's footsteps. He got out of the compulsory subjects, which students normally take. The priests recruited him for a Catholic boarding school, then he earned a scholarship to study civil engineering in America. I planned on science or medicine, too. The nuns at my American high school steered me toward physics, chemistry, and math. But my illness has never let up; it holds me back. The pills hinder my concentration and disrupt the constant effort needed for learning science. Now I prefer going into art. My aim is to be accepted to a college at the National University in Butare. People study art history, then every student picks a specialization. I would rather work

in the studio than teach. Either in painting or sculpture. I could
see getting a job in the government or opening an artist's studio in
Nyamata. I definitely don't lack the will to succeed. At some point,
the university is going to add a music department. That's my true
passion—music and dance. All different kinds: posh classical
dance, wild modern, or traditional, which is what I like the best.
I could join a troupe, take the bus to different cities, and dance in
show upon show, and why not?

My heart longs to start a family. That's the destiny of every
young Rwandan girl. There is no shortage of suitors hanging
around me. Although they make a show of gallantry, they are really
asking for love—in vain. I'm waiting for marriage. I love the beauty
of weddings, the processions of people cheered by the beautiful
outfits and giddy laughter. But I'm not impatient. As for my husband, I have no idea who he is going be. I hope that he is modest and
sensible, and has gone to university even if he spent his childhood
farming. No need for him to be rich. Too poor wouldn't do. A man
who doesn't stay late every night at the cabaret, and who isn't short,
either, relative to me. Steadfast in prayer, that would be good. His
religion doesn't matter as long as he agrees to come with me to the
church in Nyamata. Otherwise, I don't know if I could give it up.

If for some reason my mama doesn't approve of my suitor, I
will hear her out. If all he needs to do is change his habits a little,
like give up the bottle from time to time, we'll come to an understanding. I plan to listen to the arguments on both sides. A daughter
must obey her parents. But parents also have to be reasonable
when it comes to their children's true love. Their objections should
at least be legitimate, anyway.

As I said, I am not sure if I could love a Hutu boy. Would I
leave him if I happened to discover his ethnicity by surprise?
There's no simple answer. But I would prefer for my fiancé to be
a native of Nyamata, a boy who likes it here. Nyamata is growing

at a peaceful pace. In other countries, danger lurks around every corner. In Kigali, people don't care enough about those around them. The constant commotion is a real disappointment. Too many temptations. There are cases of AIDS. Young people watch sex videos before they are even fifteen years old; adults think only about big business. The city is expensive. Money eats away at friendships, the good times of youth fade away, laughter isn't heartfelt. Just too much bustle, even if Kigali has its advantages for artists. In Nyamata, people cheer each other up and lend a helping hand. And I know you've seen how much the main street has changed! New entertainment and other modern things are popping up every day in Nyamata.

Is Mama the reason I want to stay here? No, not at all, not to support her or to spend every day with close friends. I love Nyamata. It's my native land.

JEAN-PIERRE HABIMANA

NINETEEN YEARS OLD

Son of Alphonse Hitiyaremye, former Hutu prisoner

PAPA RETURNED FROM PRISON WITH STOMACH pains. They give him some trouble. So does poverty. While he was in prison, however, he learned to tell good from evil so that he will never lose his way again. His character changed. He seems more reserved. When he came home, we asked him what acts he had committed during the killings. He didn't dodge a single question, never lost his paternal temper. My mama praised him. In our home, the parents agreed together to talk about the killings, which is unthinkable in many neighbors' families.

The first question was: Why did he participate in the expeditions every day? He answered that he was following the leaders' orders, which applied throughout the hills. He told us of his comrades' warnings. Men who refused to join risked being accused of siding with the Tutsi *inkotanyi*. He described how holdouts were hit with fines. I think that it's all somewhat true. I also know that my papa doesn't offer an exhaustive truth. He skips over certain truths. Which ones? He doesn't mention that they sang during the expeditions. He says nothing about the expeditionaries' enthusiasm in the marshes—their cruelty, for example. How they would assemble an entire family, then cut them down one by one, starting with the papa first, and the mama second, so that all the children were made to watch. They would cut off tall people's legs so that their victims would see how much shorter they'd become. He zigzags through the details as soon as it is a matter of blood, if I can put it that way.

During the *gaçaças*, I listened to the witnesses. It was a big thing to hear the killings recounted under the judges' stern eyes. One day I went up to Kibungo. It was my papa's turn to be questioned. I sat down in the grass, like a spectator in the crowd. The brutality I heard filled me with indignation. I heard words surging with savage ferocity. They made me tremble with fear. They didn't seem to agree with what I knew of my papa. At home, he had told us things. But at the *gaçaça*, he described his actions, his crimes, and his victims one by one, which made me sorry and anxious and, above all, disturbed. Why disturbed? Imagining the victims' pleas beneath the blade, the wrongdoers' jeers. And fearful, too, of living with a papa who had had a hand in evil. I say it outright. Even though I have been punished with poverty and expelled from school, I still wonder about the pardon the killers received. How so? I've seen the skulls. I've been to the memorial, as I said. The rows of faded bones show the magnitude of the bloodshed. I don't know how many Tutsis he struck with his machete—he never let the expeditions leave without him. It might be a great many.

ALL THAT IS over now. I don't want to know any more. He received a pardon; he has returned to his kind self again. Deep down, I reproach him for participating in the expeditions, but age softens those feelings. He has asked his children several times to forgive him for having made a mess of their lives. He recognizes that he ruined our future. We understand, and we sincerely forgive him.

I don't encounter awkward looks when I am with my papa, because he has apologized and takes part in the community with an honest heart. He has become a good man. If he gets angry, it doesn't last. He doesn't grumble. He loves all his children equally. He stands by them, encouraging them to improve their lot despite misfortune. His crops provide his family with plenty to eat. He showed weakness, and he learned his lesson. He gets along very well with the neighbors, old or young, whatever their ethnicities. He enjoys striking up conversations with people he meets. He cracks jokes, he compliments those who deserve it. He promotes mutual aid within the cooperative of sugarcane planters and works hard organizing its raffles.

My mama doesn't keep such easy company with the neighbors. She sulks a bit and hesitates with words. The two of them work in harmony. My papa understands livestock better than my mama; he is tenacious in farming and reaps its rewards. The neighbors envy him. He currently owns four cows—milk-giving Friesian crossbreeds—and some pigs, a modern breed. He throws his energy into our banana plantation.

His gentle eyes look lovingly upon my mama. She keeps no kindness from him. They never bicker. If a problem with a child arises, he brings it to her first, for Mama became our confidante during all those years without him. She also reacts more intelligently than he does. As I said, she tried to intervene during the killings because she feared damnation. She wanted to be an honest Christian, whereas Papa thought only of the advantages of the situation. He was hot-tempered when his wife protested, and she suffered from his fits of rage. She got angry with him, she predicted his divine punishment, and then, like a good wife, she retreated.

Her name is Consolée. She holds so tightly to the truth that no one suspects her of having been mixed up in the killings. As soon as it is a matter of thinking a bit ahead, she shows more good sense. She doesn't immediately answer questions; she thinks about them first. She's a philosopher. She has confidence in her views and gives her children clear-sighted advice.

The genocide teaches us lessons that a young person would gladly do without. We use our minds dealing with the hostility between ethnicities. Dark thoughts form early on. As children, we are forced to confront extraordinary difficulties without a sound, to turn away from life's provocations. The genocide pushes us to forgo boasting and excess, to limit our desires. It spoils a child's innocence. Myself, I grew up hearing, "His papa's a big killer. He's going to kill, too, because it runs in his veins." Those words make a child shoulder burdens that are too heavy for him to bear, like hiding out in the brush or working the land though his arms lack the strength. It obliges him to pray for the sins of adults.

When a child begs God to forgive his father, he ruins his faith. He deprives himself of the right, which any other child has, to have an innocent friendship with God. Later in life, he is wary of sharing his thoughts at the cabaret with the young people his age. He watches out for the pitfalls of language. He spends his time in retreat. He doesn't dare show off in front of the girls. Why not? For fear of a hurtful remark. That's what deprived me of a university education, an exceptional future for a farmer's son. I scored good grades at school. Am I jealous of my brother at college? No, because he's my elder brother. But I scored better grades at school.

In twenty years, if the world hasn't turned completely upside down, I'll have a field and maybe five cows to improve its yield. I'll be running my own tailor's shop equipped with several Butterfly sewing machines. My ambition is to open it in Nyamata. The town is quiet, a good place to live, and suited to a fancy clientele. Would I move abroad? A well-paying job could lure me away, even if the work were exhausting. Would I leave just to try my luck—to challenge fate? No. I would go to Kigali but only for a job. Kigali is livelier, with more attractive prospects, but the poor get nothing for themselves. It's frightening.

Otherwise, I'll be back on the family plot. It grows adequate food, although the life one leads is no picnic. One doesn't get bored on the hill; there's no chance of getting bored in one's native land. In any case, you can't reproach your parents for giving birth in one place rather than another. Life is meant to be a phenomenal gift, which one accepts wherever it is offered. On the other hand, the drawbacks of growing up on a hill still matter. The world is racing toward spectacular discoveries; universities are even spreading to regional towns. Events from the wide world outside come one on top of the next. Fifteen-year-olds pull news up on the internet; they ride in airplanes. I know I'm not well informed, which is a drawback. New spots for eating fresh crops are springing up on roadsides—that's frustrating. On the hills, we have to walk kilometers to learn of the least little thing. You don't know what you don't know, and not a single neighbor knows enough to teach you. I long for change, but when none comes, its absence eats away at you.

I HAVE A girlfriend. Her name is Isabelle. We love each other. Our hearts have been entwined, I'd say, since the sweetness of childhood. She isn't too tall in stature, her skin is neither light nor dark. She's very pretty in appearance. She walks with an elegant step, and she braids her hair in the latest style. We met at school; we used to help each other review our lessons. We exchange uplifting advice. She likes ideas of all kinds; she goes looking for innovations. We joke, we laugh. She enjoys romances like the ones on television; quirky things make her smile. If she is having a good time, you know it. She's very sincere. We express our affection in both words and silence. Before, we used to meet every day, even on Sundays; we would go for strolls at the market, where we could hold hands. We exchanged sweet nothings. That doesn't happen so often anymore because of the distance—she does hair at a salon in Kigali. Now our time together depends on brief visits. We don't talk about marriage; caution keeps us quiet. Starting a family means first putting the money together to buy a house. It'll take a while given the tough spot I'm starting from. Will she be willing to wait if suitors start lining up?

Being the son of a former killer is still kind of a pain. Your heart meets suspicion, and that stifles the love and intimacy between people our age.

CHRONOLOGY OF EVENTS IN RWANDA AND IN THE DISTRICT OF NYAMATA

IN RWANDA

1921. A League of Nations mandate grants Belgium control of Rwanda.

1931. Identity cards indicating the bearer's ethnicity are introduced. They will be in use until 1994.

1961. Hutu political parties triumph in the country's first legislative elections. Rwanda is declared a republic.

1973. Major General Juvénal Habyarimana overthrows the country's first president in a coup d'état. Habyarimana will win elections allowing him to hold the presidency for the next twenty years.

1990. The Tutsi-dominated Rwandan Patriotic Front (RPF) organized at the Ugandan border achieves its first military victories against Habyarimana's troops.

1994. *April 6, 8:00 p.m.* The Hutu president Habyarimana is assassinated when his plane is shot down over the Kigali airport.

April 7, early morning. The first assassinations of key democratic figures, among whom is the Hutu prime minister Agathe Uwilingiyimana. *Interahamwe* militias invade Kigali neighborhoods. The genocide begins and will last for one hundred days. Tutsi-led RPF troops immediately begin to press into the interior of the country.

July 4. The RPF takes central Kigali.

October 3. The United Nations Security Council adopts a report classifying the massacres committed in Rwanda as genocide. According to current estimates, between eight hundred thousand and nine hundred thousand Rwandans were killed during the genocide.

1996. *November.* RPF troops carry out deadly attacks on Hutus encamped in the Kivu region of eastern Congo, forcing the return of two million Hutu refugees to Rwanda.

2001. The Rwandan government establishes the *gaçaça* courts.

IN NYAMATA

1994. *April 7–8.* Clashes between Hutus and Tutsis erupt, permanently dividing the two communities on the hills.

April 11. After four days of uncertainty, soldiers from the military base at Gako along with *interahamwe* militias begin systematic killings in the streets of Nyamata. On the hills, the local authorities muster farmers to carry out attacks on Tutsis.

April 14–15. Nearly five thousand Tutsis taking refuge in the church in Nyamata are massacred by machete. A similar number are killed in the church in Ntarama, among whom Ernestine Kaneza.

April 16. Organized hunts for Tutsis begin in the marshes and forests where Tutsis have sought refuge.

May 14. RPF troops finally reach the hills and begin searching the marshes for survivors. Fifty-one thousand corpses, out of a Tutsi population of fifty-nine thousand, are strewn in Nyamata's marshes, forests, and churches.

1996. The Hutu refugee population returns to the hills from the Kivu region. Many killers and *interahamwe* are swiftly imprisoned at the penitentiary in Rilima, around twenty kilometers from Nyamata. Among the first to be tried, Joseph-Désiré Bitero, the leader of the *interahamwe*, receives the death penalty.

2001. Trials begin for members of the Kibungo Hill gang, who receive prison sentences ranging from twelve to fifteen years.

2003. A presidential decree frees forty thousand prisoners, including all the members of the gang except for Joseph-Désiré Bitero and Élie Mizinge.

2006. The *gaçaça* courts open in Nyamata, lasting until 2010. During the trials, Ignace Rukiramacumu will be sentenced to three years of work reeducation (*travaux d'intérêt général*) and Fulgence Bunani to life imprisonment for the murder of Ernestine Kaneza.

A NOTE ABOUT THE AUTHOR

Jean Hatzfeld was born in Madagascar in 1949, and was for many years an international reporter for the French daily newspaper *Libération*. He is the author of numerous books of fiction and nonfiction, including *Life Laid Bare*, *Machete Season*, and *The Antelope's Strategy*. He lives in Paris.

A NOTE ABOUT THE TRANSLATOR

Joshua David Jordan translates twentieth- and twenty-first-century prose and poetry from the French. A specialist in the work of Henri Michaux, he teaches French literature and language at Fordham University. In 2015, he received a French Voices Award for his translation of David Lapoujade's *Aberrant Movements: The Philosophy of Gilles Deleuze*.